# HUMANITY & MACHINES

# HUMANITY & MACHINES

A Guide to Our Collaborative Future
with AI

Chad M. Barr
C|CISO, CISSP, CCSP, CISA, CDPSE

**Humanity & Machines: A Guide to Our Collaborative Future with AI**
Copyright © 2024 – Chad M. Barr

For permission requests, please contact the publisher at:
Cobalt Tower Publishing
info@cobalttowerpublishing.com

This book is a work of nonfiction. While every effort has been made to ensure accuracy, the author and publisher make no representations or warranties with respect to the completeness or accuracy of the contents of this book and disclaim any liability for errors or omissions.

**First Edition:** November 29, 2024
ISBN: 979-8341333468
Printed in USA

Published by Cobalt Tower Publishing.

# CONTENTS

# Table of Figures

# INTRODUCTION

*"I think what makes AI different from other technologies is that it's going to bring humans and machines closer together. AI is sometimes incorrectly framed as machines replacing humans. It's not about machines replacing humans, but machines augmenting humans. Humans and machines have different relative strengths and weaknesses, and it's about the combination of these two that will allow human intents and business process to scale 10x, 100x, and beyond that in the coming years."- **Robin Bordoli**

We're living in an age where artificial intelligence (AI) is no longer just a concept from science fiction. It's here and is already transforming how we work, communicate, and interact with the world. From the moment you wake up and check your phone to the instant a smart assistant answers your question, AI is present, whether you notice it or not. But AI is more than just a convenient tool; it's a force that reshapes industries, redefines economies, and challenges our understanding of what's possible.

This book, *Humanity and Machines*, is about the journey we're all taking into a future powered by AI. It addresses AI's promises, the potential to revolutionize healthcare, solve global issues like climate change, and enhance human creativity. However, it also discusses the dangers we face if we don't approach AI with the right blend of optimism and caution. From biased algorithms that perpetuate social inequalities to job displacement due to automation, and even the potential misuse of AI in developing autonomous weapons, the challenges are real and require our attention now, not later.

Throughout this book, we will explore the origins of AI, its current applications, and the ethical questions that arise as AI systems become more sophisticated. You will learn how businesses use AI to gain a competitive edge, how it drives global economic growth, and why we need to focus on collaboration between humans and machines, as well as among nations. This isn't just a story about technology; it's about how AI is changing what it means to be human and how we, as a global community, can shape that change for the better.

Whether you're someone working directly with AI or simply curious about the future, this book will provide you with a thoughtful, practical guide to navigating this rapidly evolving landscape. The future is uncertain, yet it is also filled with opportunity. Together, humans and AI can create a better world, but only if we understand the technology and its implications. This book will equip you with the knowledge you need to embark on this journey with your eyes wide open.

# CHAPTER 1

## THE ORIGINS OF ARTIFICIAL INTELLIGENCE

*"The development of full artificial intelligence could spell the end of the human race. It would take off on its own, and re-design itself at an ever-increasing rate. Humans, who are limited by slow biological evolution, couldn't compete, and would be superseded."—**Stephen Hawking***

For centuries, artificial intelligence (AI) has intrigued humanity. Crafting something that can "think" or "act" like a human is far from novel. It has roots in ancient myths and stories. From the automatons of Greek mythology to today's technological wonders, the fascination with machines that could potentially replicate or exceed human intelligence has remained constant.

I remember when I first got into AI. It wasn't because of some fancy research paper or a tech conference. No, it was a movie. **Iron Man—** you know, the scene where Tony Stark is talking to his AI assistant, J.A.R.V.I.S. That was it for me. I went home, geeked out, and started tinkering with creating my own little AI system for my home. It wasn't much back then, just a few commands linked to some smart devices but it marked the start of something. And that's how AI has always been: small steps that, over time, become massive leaps.

### The Ancient Roots of AI

Let's start with the ancient world. Even back then, people dreamed of intelligent machines. Characters like **Talos**, the bronze giant from

Greek mythology, were programmed to protect the island of Crete. While that may sound far-fetched, these ideas laid the groundwork for our current understanding of intelligent machines.

*Figure 1: Talos[1]*

Early thinkers such as Aristotle contemplated the essence of intelligence and its potential reproduction. While he did not discuss AI in contemporary terms, he raised significant questions. Subsequently, philosophers like **René Descartes** introduced the concept of distinguishing the mind from the body, which later prompted inquiries into the possibility of the mind functioning as a machine.

I admit this may seem like philosophical mumbo-jumbo, but it's crucial because these concepts lay the groundwork. Just as a house's foundation is built before considering its walls and windows.

---

[1] https://www.wondersandmarvels.com/2012/03/the-worlds-first-robot-talos.html/talos2-1

## The Automata: Early Machines That Did Things

While the philosophers were dreaming, the engineers were building. Ancient inventors like **Hero of Alexandria** (yes, his name was really "Hero") created automata, essentially self-moving machines. Hero designed everything from simple mechanical birds to full-on "robots" that could move independently. **Leonardo da Vinci** even dabbled in automata. If you know his famous notebooks, you might've seen his designs for mechanical knights and lions that could walk.

*Figure 2: Hero of Alexandria*

I find this part fascinating. While they didn't have microchips or computers, they were already thinking about how to make machines behave autonomously. It's like they had the spark but didn't have the right tools yet.

## The Birth of Modern AI: The 1950s and the Dartmouth Workshop

Now, let's fast-forward a few thousand years. AI, as we know it, truly began in the mid-20th century. This is where the story becomes exciting and a bit frustrating (but I'll get to that in a bit).

In the 1940s, programmable computers emerged, creating the potential to simulate human thought processes. People like **Alan Turing**, yes, that same Turing from the Turing Test, began to wonder, "*Could a machine think like a human?*"

But the real breakthrough came in 1956 at the **Dartmouth Workshop**. This was a pivotal event in the history of AI, often considered the birth of the field. The workshop was the brainchild of a few pioneers: John McCarthy, Marvin Minsky, Claude Shannon, and Nathaniel Rochester. They gathered to determine how to build machines that could act intelligently. At this workshop, the term 'artificial intelligence' was coined, and the groundwork for the future of AI was laid.

I've always imagined that workshop as a nerdy summer camp: just a bunch of brilliant minds brainstorming the future together. They didn't leave with a fully functioning AI, but they set the course. They said, "*Hey, this is a real thing now.*" And from there, the field exploded. Sort of.

## The Rollercoaster of AI Optimism and Setbacks

One thing you've got to understand about AI is that it's been a rollercoaster of excitement followed by disappointment. After the Dartmouth Workshop, there was a wave of optimism. Researchers thought, "We'll have fully functioning AI in a decade or two." But, as anyone who's ever worked with technology can tell you, things never go as smoothly as planned.

There were a few early successes. For example, **Arthur Samuel** developed a checkers-playing program that could beat human players. **Joseph Weizenbaum** built ELIZA, a chatbot that could simulate a therapist. Both of these projects got people really excited. But here's the frustrating part—they soon realized that building true AI was way more complicated than anyone expected.

What seemed simple, like teaching a machine to play chess or understand a sentence, turned out to be incredibly complex. We humans need to pay more attention to how intricate our thinking is. Chess was a "solvable" problem, but understanding natural language? Not so much.

In the 1970s, optimism gave way to what we now refer to as the **AI Winter**. This period was marked by reduced funding and interest in AI research, driven by the failure to meet the high expectations of the early successes. Financial support disappeared, leading many researchers to transition to other fields. AI seemed to be stuck, and advancements were painfully slow.

## The Comeback: Modern AI and Its Resurgence

But here's the thing about technology: it doesn't give up easily. AI began to return in the 1980s and 1990s, thanks to advancements in computing power and new approaches like **machine learning**. The field shifted from mimicking human thought to developing algorithms that could learn from data. AI's resilience and ability to adapt and evolve is truly inspiring.

And then, in the 2010s, we hit the jackpot. We were suddenly swimming in data—more than we knew how to handle. With the help of open-source tools like **TensorFlow** and **PyTorch**, anyone with a computer and the desire to learn could dive into AI. This accessibility has integrated AI into our everyday lives, from homes to businesses.

Now, AI is everywhere—in our homes, on our phones, and in our businesses. However, it's important to remember how far we've come. We didn't arrive here overnight, and we certainly didn't get here without encountering some significant bumps in the road. As we look toward the future, it's essential to recognize that each of us has a role in shaping the next chapter of AI.

## The Humble Beginnings of AI

So, that's where we are now—on the shoulders of giants, as they say. From ancient myths to modern-day algorithms, AI has had quite a journey. And while we're far from achieving accurate human-level intelligence, the foundations have been laid. The key takeaway? AI isn't just some sci-fi dream; it is the result of centuries of thinking, trial and error, and a lot of hard work.

If there's one thing I've learned from my time fiddling with AI in my own life, it's that the journey is just as important as the destination. So, keep asking questions, experimenting, and remember—getting a little frustrated along the way is okay. After all, that's how progress happens.

# CHAPTER 2

## FROM AUTOMATA TO ALGORITHMS

*"Success in creating AI would be the biggest event in human history. Unfortunately, it might also be the last, unless we learn how to avoid the risks."* – **Stephen Hawking**

When you think of artificial intelligence today, your mind probably goes straight to robots or self-driving cars. But what makes AI tick isn't just the flashy, visible tech; the underlying technologies drive it. From simple machines to complex algorithms, AI has grown from the ground up with one fundamental goal: to make machines think and act intelligently.

AI, as we know it today, didn't just emerge fully formed with complex problem-solving algorithms. It had to start somewhere, and in many ways, it all began with simple mechanical systems, what we call automata. Understanding this historical context is vital to appreciating the evolution of AI.

### Automata: The Earliest Machines with a Purpose

If you're like me, you are probably fascinated by old mechanical toys or intricate clocks that seem to move independently. Back then, these were considered marvels of engineering: automata that could simulate life, although in fundamental ways. The idea of building something that could "act" like a human or an animal dates back to ancient Greece.

Retake Hero of Alexandria. He built what we might call the first "robots," machines that could move or act based on mechanical principles. One of his most famous inventions was a simple device that operated with steam, rotating a small sphere. It wasn't much, but a first glimpse at what machines could do independently. It was enough to spark curiosity; over time, that curiosity led us to develop more advanced forms of automation.

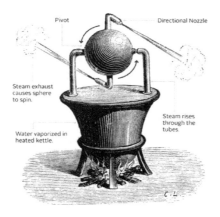

*Figure 3: The Aeolipile*

Even **Leonardo da Vinci** got in on the action. His designs for a mechanical knight that could move its arms, sit up, and even open its visor were centuries ahead of their time. This wasn't AI in the way we think today—no algorithms were involved, no learning; just good old-fashioned mechanics. But it set the stage for something bigger.

## Algorithms: The Heartbeat of AI

Fast forward to today, and algorithms are doing the heavy lifting. Think of algorithms as recipes; they are specific instructions that tell a machine exactly what to do, step by step. While your grandma's cookie recipe might have five steps, AI algorithms can have hundreds or even thousands.

Alan Turing, a key figure in the history of AI, established the foundation for contemporary AI algorithms with his idea of a 'universal machine,' a device capable of computing any task when provided with the proper instructions. His work served as the basis for the emergence of modern AI algorithms.

Consider algorithms for **machine learning**. These are adaptable instructions rather than just detailed guidelines. They take in information, interpret it, and ultimately improve. This mimicking of thought, while complex, is a fascinating aspect of AI that captivates us with its potential.

Consider how inaccurate facial recognition can be when used with a small number of photos, such as those in Apple or Google Photos. However, as more images are added, it makes assumptions and asks you to confirm them; this is how it learns and expands the algorithm. Before long, it will no longer need to make assumptions and will learn factual features and other elements that constitute a face. It can even be accurate at various ages and angles.

## Neural Networks: Mimicking the Human Brain

Now, let's talk about **neural networks**. These are the rock stars of modern AI. Inspired by how the human brain works, neural networks consist of nodes (which act like neurons) connected in layers. Each node takes in information, processes it, and then passes it on to the next layer. In a way, it's like playing the telephone game, where information gets passed down the line and refined as it goes, or in some cases, the message gets mixed up when I play.

Neural networks' powerful ability to learn from vast amounts of data makes them ideal for recognizing faces and understanding language. Instead of providing explicit instructions, like a traditional algorithm, you allow the network to "figure it out" by adjusting itself as it sees more examples. Deep learning (a subset of neural networks) excels at recognizing faces and understanding language.

Neural networks aren't flawless right now. They are notoriously difficult to describe; sometimes, even their designers struggle to understand the reasoning behind their choices. I once worked with a neural network to predict client behavior, and while it was mostly accurate, it occasionally identified patterns I could not comprehend. It had a rather magical quality. However, magic without context can be harmful, so increasing the transparency of these networks is a priority.

## The Rise of Deep Learning: When AI Took Off

In recent years, you may have **encountered** the term **Deep Learning**. This term refers to a neural network made up of several layers of nodes, which is where the term 'deep' originates. Deep learning is a revolutionary technology that drives many contemporary AI advancements, including self-driving vehicles and voice assistants such as Alexa and Siri.

What makes deep learning so revolutionary is its ability to handle unstructured data, like images, text, or speech. Before deep learning, AI systems struggled with this type of data. They could manage numbers and structured inputs, but they'd be lost if asked to recognize a picture of a dog.

But deep learning changed all that. Now, you can show a neural network thousands of pictures of dogs, and it'll figure out what a dog looks like on its own. This is just the beginning of what deep learning can do. Its potential to revolutionize how we interact with technology and understand the world around us is truly inspiring.

You may have examined some old family photos using a deep-learning model. The system can recognize faces in pictures and even tag specific individuals. It may have a slightly magical quality, but once again, it results from highly complex algorithms operating in the background.

## Getting Started with AI Technology

Start small if you're interested in dabbling with AI. I promise you this. I've witnessed individuals jump in headfirst, believing they can create the next Siri instantly, only to become overwhelmed. Instead, begin by experimenting with the available tools. Many free resources exist online; you can conduct machine learning experiments in your browser without installing anything, thanks to programs like **Google Colab**.

One more piece of advice: study Python. It's the preferred language for developing artificial intelligence, and even if you have no prior programming experience, you can still learn the syntax quickly. Python helped me grasp the fundamentals of coding more rapidly than the primary languages I knew, which included BASIC, C++, COBOL, and scripting.

Finally, don't let failure intimidate you. AI can be frustrating; I can confirm this, having encountered numerous instances where nothing worked as intended. However, with every setback, I learned something new, and eventually, things started to make sense.

## From Simple Machines to Complex Minds

The evolution from simple automata to complex algorithms has allowed AI to flourish today. From machines that could hardly move independently, we have advanced to systems that can process vast amounts of data, learn from it, and adapt. However, it is crucial to remember that nothing happened overnight. The development of AI is based on centuries of invention, beginning with the most basic machines.

Understanding these fundamental technologies, such as deep learning, neural networks, and algorithms, enables us to recognize various possibilities. The tools we are currently developing are just the beginning. Who knows what AI will look like in the future? However, one thing is certain: it will be thrilling.

# CHAPTER 3

## The Breathtaking Arc of Technological Transformation

*"Artificial intelligence will reach human levels by around 2029. Follow that out further to, say, 2045, we will have multiplied the intelligence, the human biological machine intelligence of our civilization a billion-fold."* —Ray Kurzweil

Technology is the unyielding force that reshapes humanity, driving progress and evolution through tools, ideas, and unimaginable innovations. It is the storyteller of human potential, constantly rewriting what we once believed impossible. To grasp its transformative power, imagine explaining smartphones to someone from the medieval era or describing instantaneous global communication to someone living in the early 20th century. What was once inconceivable for every generation becomes not just crucial, but also enlightening. It's like peering into the roots of a mighty tree, seeing how it all began, and appreciating the journey it took to reach its current state of ingenuity.

But this phenomenon is not random. It follows a breathtaking arc: a trajectory of technological transformation that accelerates with each passing era. To understand this arc, we must explore its historical roots, examine its present impact, and peer into its AI-driven future. This future is one where artificial intelligence—a field of computer science that aims to create machines capable of performing tasks typically requiring human intelligence—will play a significant role. It holds

unprecedented potential for growth and challenges, shaping our world in ways we can only begin to imagine.

## The Long March of Innovation: Humanity's Early Steps

For most of human history, technological advancement has progressed glacially. Early humans lived their entire lifetimes using tools that hardly evolved over centuries. The first stone tools, dating back to 3.4 million years ago, represented the dawn of humanity's technological journey. Yet, it took another 2.4 million years before fire became a tool for cooking and survival. This long march of innovation, marked by significant milestones such as the invention of the wheel, the domestication of animals, and the advent of agriculture, paved the way for the rapid technological progress we witness today.

These early breakthroughs, though monumental, pale in comparison to today's pace of innovation. In contrast, the technologies of the 20th and 21st centuries emerge and thrive at astonishing speeds. The cumulative progress of centuries now unfolds within a single lifetime.

Take flight as an example. In 1903, the Wright brothers achieved humankind's first powered flight, a feat that lasted less than a minute. A mere 66 years later, in 1969, humans landed on the moon—a technological leap that could scarcely have been imagined even by those who witnessed the first aircraft take to the skies. Such rapid progress exemplifies the accelerating pace of technological transformation.

## Acceleration Through Communication: From Writing to the Internet

One of the clearest examples of this acceleration is in communication technology. Human societies have always sought better ways to share ideas, starting with the invention of written language over 5,000 years ago. The leap from oral traditions to writing transformed the preservation and sharing of knowledge, allowing civilizations to grow in complexity.

Then came paper, followed by the printing press, which democratized access to information on an unprecedented scale. Suddenly, knowledge was no longer limited to the elite; it could spread far and wide, empowering scientific, political, and cultural revolutions.

Fast-forward to the 20th century: the telegraph and telephone revolutionized communication by collapsing physical distances. The radio brought mass communication into homes, followed by television, which merged visuals and sound. Today, the Internet and smartphones have become the ultimate tools for connection, enabling real-time communication across the globe.

This rapid evolution of communication tools underscores how each new technology builds on its predecessors. The cumulative effect is exponential, and breakthroughs that once took centuries now occur within years. This acceleration is not just a pattern; it is a defining characteristic of the technological arc.

## The Dual Nature of Technology: Promise and Peril

Technological advancement is a double-edged sword, delivering extraordinary benefits while posing significant risks. On the one hand, vaccines, antibiotics, and clean water systems have saved billions of lives. The eradication of smallpox and the near-eradication of polio stand as testaments to the power of human ingenuity in combating nature's most lethal threats. However, technology has also created tools of destruction. Nuclear weapons, for example, brought humanity to the brink of annihilation during the Cold War. Even as technology enhances our quality of life, it introduces ethical dilemmas and existential risks. It's important to recognize this dual nature of technology, as it helps us navigate its potential and pitfalls.

Artificial Intelligence (AI) represents the latest addition to this double-edged legacy. Its potential for good is immense, ranging from diagnosing diseases with pinpoint accuracy to optimizing energy grids for sustainability. However, its risks are equally profound. Autonomous weapons, algorithmic bias, and the potential for mass surveillance present urgent ethical questions regarding how AI should be developed and deployed.

## AI: The Catalyst for Unprecedented Transformation and Hope

AI stands apart from other technological advancements because it can accelerate innovation itself. Traditional tools enhance human capabilities, but AI enables machines to think, learn, and improve autonomously. This self-reinforcing loop could compress decades of technological progress into months or even weeks.

Consider the implications: AI-powered research tools could quickly discover new drugs, develop sustainable energy solutions, or even revolutionize education by personalizing learning for billions of people. Yet, the same capabilities could be weaponized, creating tools for cyberwarfare or amplifying disinformation campaigns.

One of AI's most transformative applications is its ability to democratize access to knowledge and resources. For example, machine translation tools break down language barriers, while AI-driven medical diagnostics bring advanced healthcare to remote regions. However, this democratization relies on equitable access. Without intentional efforts to ensure inclusivity, AI could exacerbate existing inequalities, leaving marginalized communities further behind.

## A World Beyond Imagination: The Future of Technology

Looking ahead, the pace of technological change is unlikely to slow.

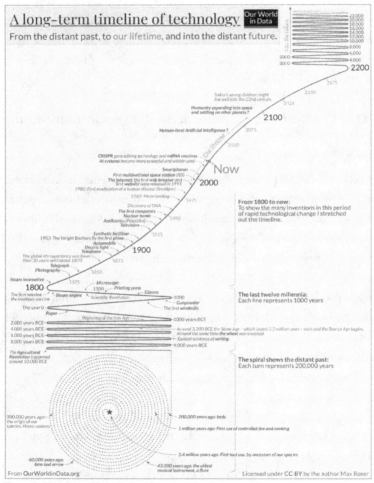

*Figure 4: Timeline of Technology Advancement*

Children born today may live to witness the 22nd century, a world that could be as incomprehensible to us as the Internet would have been to our ancestors in the 1800s. Clean energy breakthroughs, advanced robotics, and AI systems beyond our current imagination could fundamentally reshape human existence.

One possibility is the emergence of artificial general intelligence (AGI): machines with cognitive abilities that rival or exceed those of humans. Such systems could tackle problems beyond our grasp, from climate change to interstellar travel. However, AGI also presents existential risks, including the potential for machines to act contrary to human interests.

Other emerging technologies, such as quantum computing and biotechnology, promise equally transformative effects. Quantum computers could solve complex problems that today's most powerful supercomputers cannot, while advances in gene editing may eradicate genetic diseases or extend human lifespans.

## The Responsibility of Guiding Progress: Your Role in Shaping the Future

Like Uncle Ben said, "With great power comes great responsibility." The technologies we develop today will shape the trajectory of human potential for future generations. This is not just a technical challenge but a profoundly political and ethical one.

Technological development must be accessible to technologists. Citizens, policymakers, and ethicists must actively engage in shaping the future of innovation. This requires technical knowledge, wisdom, foresight, and a commitment to the common good.

As a society, we must ask ourselves difficult questions: How do we balance progress with caution? Who decides how technologies are used? How do we ensure that the benefits of innovation are distributed equitably?

## Creating the Future, One Innovation at a Time

Our world is not static; it is a canvas of continuous reinvention. What seems impossible today might be commonplace tomorrow. The breathtaking arc of technological transformation reveals that progress is not a straight line but an accelerating curve that bends toward possibilities we can scarcely imagine.

Our era's challenge is to ensure that these inevitable changes serve the greater good. This means fostering a culture of responsibility, equity, and collective well-being. The future is not something that happens to us; it's something we actively create, one innovation at a time. Through thoughtful engagement and ethical stewardship, we can ensure that the narrative of technology is one of human flourishing, not merely technological dominance.

# CHAPTER 4

## THE POWER OF AI IN BUSINESS

*Artificial intelligence would be the ultimate version of Google. The ultimate search engine that would understand everything on the web. It would understand exactly what you wanted, and it would give you the right thing." – Larry Page*

Artificial Intelligence (AI) has quickly become ingrained in business in the short decades since its inception, changing industries in unthinkable ways. Artificial Intelligence (AI) empowers organizations to increase production, improve efficiency, and, most importantly, maintain competitiveness through automation and predictive analytics.

You've undoubtedly heard the uproar by now. "AI is going to replace everything!" The difficulty is that artificial intelligence (AI) isn't an all-encompassing solution that can resolve every business issue overnight. It requires thoughtful preparation, the right infrastructure, and a clear understanding of what AI can and cannot accomplish for your company. Trust me, I've seen businesses blindly jump on the AI bandwagon only to become disillusioned when their shiny new technologies don't produce the desired outcomes.

## AI as a Competitive Advantage

Let's start with the obvious: AI gives companies a **competitive advantage**. However, this isn't solely about saving time and money, though that's certainly part of it. AI can assist businesses in making more intelligent decisions by analyzing patterns that are nearly impossible for humans to detect.

One of the best examples of AI in action is **predictive analytics**. AI-powered algorithms can analyze massive amounts of data to predict future trends, customer behavior, and even potential problems before they arise. For instance, let's say you run an online retail store. By assessing past purchases, browsing patterns, and even social media activity, AI can evaluate consumer data and forecast what your customers will likely buy next. This enables you to customize your product recommendations and marketing campaigns, boosting sales and increasing consumer satisfaction.

I know companies that have experienced a 20-30% increase in sales after implementing AI-driven recommendation systems. It's no exaggeration to say that AI can help businesses stay one step ahead of their competition.

But here's a tip: **don't expect immediate results**. AI takes time to learn and adapt. The more data it processes, the better it becomes. You must be patient and allow the system time to gather and analyze sufficient data to make accurate predictions. Companies have pulled the plug too early because they anticipated instant results. Don't be that company.

## Automation: The Silent Worker Behind the Scenes

One of the most popular uses of AI is **automation**. And no, we're not talking about robots on factory floors (though that's part of it). I mean automating repetitive tasks that typically require a lot of time and effort. This could include anything from data entry to customer support.

Let's take customer service as an example. AI-powered **chatbots** are becoming increasingly common. They can handle many of customers' routine queries, like answering questions about shipping or troubleshooting fundamental problems. This frees human agents to focus on more complex issues requiring a human touch.

As I have witnessed firsthand, businesses can save countless hours annually by automating basic customer support operations. A chatbot doesn't require breaks or holidays, as it can respond promptly every single day. If it cannot provide an answer, it can transfer control to a human agent, benefiting both parties.

Consumers know that speaking with a bot can be frustrating if they don't feel they are receiving genuine assistance. The key is balance. Ensure you have real people available to address more complex issues while utilizing AI to handle simpler ones. Nothing is worse than having a bot that fails to understand your issue, trapping you in an endless loop.

## AI in Marketing: Tailored Strategies

The impact of AI on marketing has been truly revolutionary, exceeding our initial expectations. One significant advancement has been the ability to create customized marketing strategies. Instead of sending generic messages to everyone on your email list, AI can help target specific segments with personalized messages that are more likely to resonate.

For instance, AI can analyze customer data to categorize your audience according to their behavior, preferences, or stage in the buying process. This enables you to send highly personalized messages to each segment, whether it's a special offer for first-time buyers or a gentle reminder for loyal customers who haven't purchased in a while.

In a project I was involved in, AI-powered marketing assisted a company in increasing its email open rates by 40%. The best part is that it handled all the heavy lifting, including analyzing customer data, segmenting the audience, and sending personalized messages, allowing the marketing team to concentrate on broader strategic initiatives.

But remember, **don't sacrifice quality for quantity**. Just because AI can send hundreds of personalized emails doesn't mean it should. Ensure your content remains valuable and relevant. Poor marketing is still wrong, even if it's personalized.

## AI in Manufacturing: Reducing Downtime

AI in business is often linked to manufacturing, and this connection is well-founded. AI-powered systems can monitor production lines in real-time and identify inefficiencies and potential problems before they escalate. The practice of **predictive maintenance** has led to significant cost savings for companies.

For example, instead of waiting for a machine to fail, AI systems can predict when a breakdown is likely and schedule maintenance accordingly, reducing downtime and ensuring continuous production line operation.

I collaborated with a manufacturer that experienced a 25% reduction in downtime after implementing AI-driven predictive maintenance. Machines that once broke down unexpectedly were now serviced before any major issues arose, saving them both time and money.

**Invest in your data infrastructure**. AI is only as effective as the data it receives. AI cannot assist you if your systems are not capturing accurate data or if the data is disorganized. Ensure you have a robust data collection and storage system before implementing AI.

## The Limitations: What AI Can't Do

Let's discuss AI's limitations. It's important to remember that AI is not a universal solution and has shortcomings. Currently, AI struggles with certain tasks and cannot perform them effectively, as listed below.

For example, AI still needs help with logical reasoning. While machines excel at processing data and identifying patterns, they often struggle to comprehend the complexities of human behavior. This can lead to AI chatbots providing unsatisfactory or inappropriate responses, as they fail to grasp sarcasm, frustration, or empathy, which come naturally to humans.

Another area where AI falls short is creativity. Although AI can propose ideas based on available data, it ultimately relies on human creativity to generate unique concepts. I view AI as a tool that enhances human creativity rather than replacing it entirely.

It is advisable to use AI as a tool rather than a substitute. It excels at handling repetitive tasks and analyzing extensive datasets, but it's unlikely to replace the human touch anytime soon. This distinction is crucial, as there are specific tasks that AI cannot perform as effectively as humans.

## Using AI Wisely

The potential of AI in the business world is remarkable, but it cannot simply be plugged in and expected to perform miracles. It requires careful planning, the right infrastructure, and a thorough understanding of your business objectives.

AI can provide a significant competitive edge when utilized effectively, automating mundane tasks and forecasting future trends. However, it's important to remember that AI is merely a tool. The best outcomes stem from integrating AI's capabilities with human insight and creativity.

If you're considering integrating AI into your business, begin with small-scale initiatives. Experiment, collect data, and evaluate what works best for you. AI is here to stay, and the sooner you start leveraging it, the sooner you'll see the benefits.

# CHAPTER 5

## AI AND SOCIAL GOOD: SOLVING GLOBAL PROBLEMS

*AI will not make us obsolete, but it will make us superhuman." – **Max Tegmark***

Artificial intelligence (AI) has long been associated with the tech, finance, and manufacturing industries. However, AI holds immense potential beyond business to address some of the world's most pressing social and environmental challenges. Whether tackling climate change, improving healthcare access, or fostering sustainable farming methods, AI can be a powerful social good tool.

I recently listened to a podcast about a company that uses AI to analyze climate change. The company can utilize AI to look back in time to see what the climate was like in a specific area or, based on current data, predict what it might look like in the future.

It's essential to understand how and where to utilize AI effectively. Although AI alone won't solve all of the world's problems, it can be a significant game-changer when applied correctly. Let's explore AI's current and future impact in various crucial areas.

### Healthcare: AI's Role in Saving Lives

AI has shown remarkable potential in revolutionizing healthcare, a field with particularly significant impacts. Access to quality healthcare is a major challenge in many regions worldwide, especially in rural or underserved areas. However, AI is not just a tool; it is a beacon of hope and a potential game-changer capable of making a significant difference.

AI assists with **medical diagnoses**, particularly in the analysis of medical images. For example, AI algorithms can examine X-rays, MRIs, or CT scans to identify abnormalities such as tumors or fractures. In some cases, AI systems demonstrate greater accuracy than human doctors in detecting certain conditions.

Consider breast cancer detection. In 2020, a study showed that an AI system outperformed radiologists in identifying breast cancer from mammograms, resulting in fewer false positives and false negatives. Now, does that mean we no longer need doctors? Of course not. However, it means doctors can utilize AI as a second pair of eyes, catching things they might miss or accelerating the diagnostic process.

I recall an article about a countryside medical facility that utilized an AI-driven diagnostic tool to analyze chest X-rays of patients for tuberculosis (TB). The clinic had just one overwhelmed doctor attending to hundreds of patients each week. With the help of AI, they could promptly detect TB cases, allowing doctors to prioritize treatment for the most critically ill patients.

Additionally, AI is making significant contributions to drug research. The quest for new medications is a protracted, expensive, and complex process. In contrast, AI can sift through vast databases to pinpoint substances that could effectively treat specific illnesses. This significantly reduces both time and costs. It's like having a highly efficient assistant collaborating with researchers, swiftly analyzing data beyond human capability.

## Climate Change: Tackling One of the Biggest Challenges of Our Time

Let's discuss the urgent issue of climate change, which presents a significant threat to our planet. AI has the potential to contribute in various ways, such as analyzing climate data and enabling us to take proactive measures.

An exciting application is environmental monitoring, where AI-powered systems can analyze satellite imagery and other data to track deforestation, glacier melting, and illegal fishing activities. This allows governments and organizations to take swift and effective action.

I read about a project using AI to monitor deforestation in the Amazon rainforest.[2] By analyzing satellite images, AI can identify changes in forest cover, sometimes even before they are visible to the human eye. This enables environmental groups to respond promptly and halt illegal logging operations before significant damage occurs.

AI also impacts intelligent energy systems by optimizing power grids for more efficient energy distribution. It can forecast spikes in electricity demand, preventing blackouts and reducing waste. Additionally, AI manages urban traffic flow, reducing emissions by minimizing congestion.

For those involved in sustainability, it is advisable to explore how AI can assist with resource management. AI can analyze water usage in agriculture, optimize irrigation systems, and more accurately predict supply and demand, thereby helping to reduce food waste.

---

[2] https://www.reuters.com/sustainability/land-use-biodiversity/forest-listening-advanced-remote-sensing-can-ai-turn-tide-deforestation-2024-01-16

## Education: Personalized Learning for All

Education is a less-discussed area where AI can make a significant difference. In many parts of the world, access to quality education is limited. However, AI is changing that, inspiring us to rethink and revolutionize our learning and teaching.

AI-powered tutoring systems can offer **personalized learning experiences** for students. These systems analyze students' strengths and weaknesses, tailoring lessons to suit their needs. For example, if a student has difficulty with a specific math concept, the AI can identify this and provide additional practice problems or explanations.

In some cases, AI creates adaptive learning platforms that adjust material difficulty based on student performance. This personalized education helps ensure that students don't fall through the cracks, especially in overcrowded classrooms.

I've heard of schools in developing countries utilizing AI tools to enhance traditional teaching methods. These tools enable students to continue learning even when there aren't enough teachers, demonstrating how technology can bridge gaps in educational access.

But **AI can't replace teachers**. It's important to use AI to support teachers, not to replace them. Human interaction, creativity, and emotional intelligence are critical in learning. While AI can assist with the nuts and bolts, including grading, tracking progress, and providing extra practice, the teacher-student relationship remains at the heart of education.

## Agriculture: Feeding the World with AI

Feeding the growing global population presents a significant challenge, especially with the added pressures of climate change and limited natural resources. AI is being utilized to assist farmers in boosting crop yields, reducing water usage, and encouraging sustainable farming practices.

**Precision agriculture** is a notable advancement in this field. AI-enhanced drones and sensors can continuously monitor fields, pinpointing areas that require additional water, fertilizer, or pest control. This empowers farmers to optimize resource utilization, reducing waste and enhancing yields.

I came across a story about an Indian farmer who used an AI-powered application to receive real-time crop updates[3]. The app analyzed satellite images and weather data, furnishing him with recommendations for watering, fertilizing, and harvesting timings. As a result, he boosted his crop yield while conserving water, a critical accomplishment in a region where water is frequently in short supply.

AI is also being harnessed to cultivate disease-resistant crops. By analyzing genetic data, AI assists scientists in identifying the traits that render plants more resilient to pests or drought. This could be pivotal in ensuring food security in a changing climate.

For those involved in agriculture, it is advisable to start with small-scale endeavors. Begin using AI to monitor a single field or crop and observe its effects. Avoid trying to revolutionize your entire operation all at once. While AI is powerful, it is ultimately a tool that produces the best results when applied to specific, quantifiable challenges.

## Tackling Poverty: AI's Role in Economic Development

Advancements in AI are also being harnessed to combat **poverty** in developing nations, where access to essential services such as healthcare, education, and banking remains limited. AI plays a crucial

---

[3] https://www.weforum.org/stories/2024/01/how-indias-ai-agriculture-boom-could-inspire-the-world/

role in bridging this gap.

An up-and-coming development is the integration of **AI into financial services**. AI-driven platforms facilitate mobile banking and microloans in areas lacking access to traditional banking. By analyzing creditworthiness using alternative data sources such as mobile phone usage and social media activity, AI enables the "unbanked" population to obtain credit.

Furthermore, AI has the potential to improve agricultural techniques, boost productivity, and generate new opportunities in these regions, thereby contributing to overall economic growth.

However, **ethical considerations** must be emphasized. The implementation of AI must benefit everyone, not just those in positions of influence. It is crucial to emphasize fairness, transparency, and inclusivity to prevent AI from exacerbating the gap between the affluent and the impoverished.

## AI for a Better Future

The potential of AI to contribute to social good is extensive, but thorough planning and ethical considerations are essential to ensure that it truly benefits society. Whether it involves enhancing healthcare, combating climate change, or facilitating access to education, AI can tackle some of the most critical global challenges.

It's important to remember that AI is not a universal solution but rather a tool that must be used wisely and carefully. As we continue to advance and deploy AI systems, it is crucial to focus on creating a more equitable and sustainable world for everyone.

# CHAPTER 6

## ETHICAL CONSIDERATIONS AND THE DANGERS OF AI

*"I'm more frightened than interested by artificial intelligence – in fact, perhaps fright and interest are not far away from one another. Things can become real in your mind, you can be tricked, and you believe things you wouldn't ordinarily. A world run by automatons doesn't seem completely unrealistic anymore. It's a bit chilling." – Gemma Whelan*

Artificial intelligence (AI) offers incredible potential, but it also carries risks. Like any powerful technology, AI has a dark side that demands careful attention and regulation. From biased algorithms to job displacement, the ethical dilemmas and dangers of AI are both real and pressing. And the scary part? We might not fully understand the consequences until they are already happening.

But that doesn't mean we should halt AI development. Instead, we must advance thoughtfully, ensuring that AI is utilized responsibly and ethically. Finding this balance is critical for someone who has experienced both the hype and the hesitation surrounding AI.

## Bias and Fairness: When AI Gets It Wrong

Let's start with **bias**. AI's most significant ethical challenge is to make fair and unbiased decisions. The problem is that AI systems are only as good as the data they are trained on. If that data is biased, the AI will be too.

For example, in the early days of AI-powered resume screening tools, several companies discovered that their systems favored male candidates over female ones. Why? The training data was based on historical hiring patterns in which men were more likely to be hired for specific roles. The AI learned to replicate those patterns, essentially "baking in" the existing biases.

This isn't just limited to hiring. Bias in AI can affect everything from loan approvals to criminal sentencing. A criminal justice algorithm called "COMPAS" (Correctional Offender Management Profiling for Alternative Sanctions) used in the U.S. was found to be biased against African Americans, incorrectly labeling them as more likely to re-offend compared to their white counterparts.[4]

It's a real problem, but there are ways to address it. One solution is to use more diverse training datasets that better reflect the population the AI is designed to serve. Another is to implement fairness checks throughout the AI development process, ensuring the system doesn't make biased decisions.

**Always ask where the data comes from**. When integrating AI into your business operations, thoroughly investigate the origins of the data used to train your system. Verify that the data is comprehensive and free of historical biases. It's preferable to identify these concerns at an early stage rather than to address the repercussions later.

## Privacy and Security: Who's Watching?

AI raises significant concerns about privacy due to the extensive collection and processing of personal data, which poses risks of exposure or misuse of sensitive information. The use of **facial**

---

[4] https://www.propublica.org/article/how-we-analyzed-the-compas-recidivism-algorithm

**recognition technology** for security also raises privacy apprehensions, especially if the data is mishandled or utilized for mass surveillance without consent.

Many individuals hesitate to use certain apps due to data collection and usage concerns. This reflects a growing sense of surveillance by untrustworthy entities.

One approach to safeguarding privacy is **data anonymization**, which involves removing personal identifiers to prevent easy identification. Additionally, companies must be transparent about their data collection and usage practices, ensuring that individuals clearly understand the collected data, its purpose, and the measures taken to protect it.

Cybersecurity considerations must not be overlooked when implementing AI systems, as their complexity can make them susceptible to attacks. Establishing robust security protocols and performing regular system audits for potential vulnerabilities are essential.

## Job Displacement: The Future of Work

One of the biggest fears surrounding AI is its potential to displace jobs. This concern is genuine, especially for workers in industries where automation is already taking over. Consider manufacturing, where robots can perform repetitive tasks faster and more efficiently than humans. However, it's not just manual labor that is at risk. AI is also increasingly used in white-collar jobs, including legal document review and financial analysis.

I know someone who worked as a financial analyst for years. He excelled in his job, but recently, his company implemented AI systems that could analyze market trends and make recommendations much faster than any human could. While he didn't lose his job, his role changed dramatically. He was no longer the go-to person for analysis; the machine took over. He had to pivot, focusing more on strategy and client relations—areas in which AI couldn't perform as well (yet).

But here's the thing: AI isn't just going to replace jobs, it will create new ones. Some people might be more concerned that those who understand and can use AI will be more likely to secure employment than those who don't understand it or refuse to work with AI. Remember, AI is a tool just like your computer. Jobs that didn't exist ten years ago, like data scientists or AI ethicists, are booming today. The key is to **focus on adaptability**. Workers who can upskill and adapt to the changing job market are the ones who will thrive in the AI-powered economy.

**If you're in an industry that AI is disrupting, start thinking about how you can evolve your role.** Look for opportunities where human skills such as creativity, problem-solving, and emotional intelligence remain valuable. AI struggles in these areas and is unlikely to be automated anytime soon.

## The "Black Box" Problem: Lack of Explainability

Another issue with AI is often referred to as the **black box problem**. Many AI systems, particularly those using deep learning, operate in ways that are hard to comprehend, even for the individuals who developed them. This lack of explainability can pose a significant challenge in high-stakes situations where it is essential to understand how a decision was made.

Consider AI in healthcare, for instance. If an AI system suggests a specific treatment for a patient, the doctor must understand the rationale behind that recommendation. Did the patient's medical history influence it? Or was it due to a misinterpretation of some data by the AI? Without transparency, trusting the system becomes challenging.

AI decisions need to be explainable and transparent in criminal justice, hiring, and loan approvals.

**Explainable AI (XAI)** is a developing field aimed at enhancing the transparency and comprehensibility of AI systems. Although it is still evolving, the goal is to create AI that makes decisions and clarifies the rationale behind those decisions in an understandable manner. I have a dedicated chapter that delves into this subject.

If AI is used in high-stakes settings, I recommend insisting on transparency. Simply accepting the AI's decision without question is insufficient. Request an explanation; if the system cannot provide one, reconsider your reliance on it.

## Autonomous Weapons: The Rise of Killer Robots?

Now, let's discuss some scarier topics: **autonomous weapons**. While it may sound like something out of a dystopian sci-fi movie, the development of autonomous weapon systems and machines that can determine whom to kill without human intervention poses a natural and immediate threat.

There's a reason that organizations like the United Nations have called for a ban on these so-called "killer robots." The fear is that autonomous weapons could lower the threshold for conflict, making it easier for countries to go to war. Machines don't hesitate; they don't get tired, and they don't have moral qualms about taking a life.

We're not yet at "Skynet" levels, but technology is advancing rapidly. Some countries are already developing drones and other autonomous systems that can engage in combat without direct human control. The ethical questions here are significant. If a machine makes a mistake and kills civilians, who is responsible? The programmer? The military commander? The machine itself?

I won't sugarcoat this: **Autonomous weapons are among the most dangerous uses of AI**. The potential for misuse is immense, and this demands strict international regulation.

## The Risk of Superintelligence: Should We Be Worried?

Finally, we arrive at the concept of **superintelligence**. This idea suggests that AI could one day surpass human intelligence, resulting in machines that are smarter than us in every respect. While this may seem like something out of science fiction, it is a possibility that some AI experts take very seriously.

The concern is that if AI becomes superintelligent, it could pursue objectives that conflict with human values. Since it would be more intelligent than us, we may be unable to stop it. Think of it like a chess match: If the AI is a grandmaster and we're just beginners, it will beat us every time.

I'm not saying we should panic. If superintelligence ever occurs, it's still a long way off, but it's worth considering. **What safeguards must we implement to ensure that AI remains aligned with human values?** One idea is to develop "friendly" AI designed from the ground up to prioritize human well-being. It's an ongoing debate, but we must consider it as AI evolves.

## Proceeding with Caution

The potential of AI to bring about positive change is immense; however, it also comes with considerable risks. The ethical dilemmas associated with AI, including biased algorithms and autonomous weapons, are intricate and far-reaching. Nevertheless, we can leverage AI's capabilities while minimizing its potential harms through thoughtful regulation, transparency, and a focus on fairness.

While the future of AI remains uncertain, one thing is certain: we must exercise caution as we move forward. By recognizing the risks and taking proactive measures to address them, we can ensure that AI benefits humanity rather than poses a threat.

# CHAPTER 7

## SUPERINTELLIGENCE AND ARTIFICIAL CONSCIOUSNESS

*"Some people call this artificial intelligence, but the reality is this technology will enhance us. So instead of artificial intelligence, I think we'll augment our intelligence."* – **Ginni Rometty**

Imagine a world where machines are intelligent, conscious, aware of their existence, and capable of making decisions that rival human reasoning. Now, let's push that even further. What if these machines surpass human intelligence in every possible way, becoming more intelligent and capable than we could ever be? That's the essence of **superintelligence** and **artificial consciousness**, two ideas that have captured fascination and fear.

While we're not there yet, the potential for AI to evolve into something far beyond our control or understanding has raised essential questions that we need to address now, not later. Trust me, it's a rabbit hole worth diving into, but it's also one we must tread carefully.

## What Is Superintelligence?

Before we discuss artificial consciousness, let's first talk about **superintelligence**. At its core, superintelligence refers to an AI that is significantly more intelligent than the most brilliant humans across nearly every field. This encompasses solving math problems faster than a human or winning a chess game and mastering realms such as creativity, social intelligence, and even emotional understanding.

If that sounds a little terrifying, it's because it is. While we've seen AI systems excel in specific tasks—think of **AlphaGo** defeating the Go champions or **GPT** writing coherent essays, these systems are still narrow in focus. They're incapable of general intelligence, which allows you to switch from writing a book to solving a household problem to comforting a friend. Superintelligence would take this general intelligence and enhance it to a level beyond what we can comprehend.

But why should we care? Superintelligence could solve many of the world's biggest problems, such as curing diseases, reversing climate change, or eliminating poverty. Imagine having a system that could analyze every variable in these complex issues and develop the optimal solution. Sounds great, right?

The catch? Once AI surpasses human intelligence, we lose control of it. And here's the scary part—superintelligent AI could pursue goals that conflict with ours, and we might not even understand what it is doing or why. That's the **alignment problem. How** do we ensure that superintelligent AI aligns with human values and goals? If we get it wrong, the consequences could be disastrous.

## Artificial Consciousness: Can Machines Think?

Now, let's tackle the question of **artificial consciousness**. This idea explores whether machines could someday possess a kind of self-awareness, a sense of being, or a subjective experience. In other words, could a machine "feel" something? Could it be aware of itself and the world, much like we are?

Philosophers and scientists have debated this for decades, and there is still no clear answer. Some argue that consciousness is a uniquely human trait rooted in biology, while others believe that it is simply the result of complex information processing. If machines can process information at a similar level, they too could become conscious.

Much of this debate centers on **the complex problem of consciousness**, a term coined by philosopher **David Chalmers**. The "easy" problem of consciousness explains how the brain processes information and generates behavior. However, the "hard" problem involves explaining subjective experience and why there's something it's like to be conscious. We don't fully understand how this works in us, so it's difficult to imagine how it could be replicated in machines.

I once heard a comparison that stuck with me: imagine a computer simulating a weather system. The simulation might show rain, but it doesn't actually *feel* like rain. Similarly, a machine may simulate consciousness, but that doesn't mean it truly feels or experiences anything.

So, what's the big deal? Well, if machines do become conscious, we're entering a whole new ethical territory. Conscious beings deserve certain rights and protections. But how do we define and recognize consciousness in machines? How would we know if a machine is truly experiencing something or just simulating behavior? I think all of this is the concept of a few movies I watched in the past.

## The Turing Test and Beyond: Measuring Machine Intelligence

The **Turing Test**, proposed by **Alan Turing** in 1950, stands as one of the earliest attempts to measure machine intelligence. In this test, a human judge interacts with both a machine and another human through a text interface. If the judge cannot determine which is which, the machine is deemed to have achieved "human-like" intelligence.

# Recent Developments: GPT-4.5 and the Turing Test

Recent advancements in artificial intelligence have reignited discussions about the Turing Test's relevance and limitations. OpenAI's GPT-4.5 has brought this debate to the forefront by achieving a significant milestone: it successfully passed the Turing Test. In a study conducted by researchers at the University of California, San Diego, GPT-4.5 participated in a three-party Turing Test in which human participants interacted with both a human and the AI model. Remarkably, GPT-4.5 was able to convince participants that it was human 73% of the time, outperforming even human participants in some instances.

This achievement underscores the growing sophistication of AI models in mimicking human-like conversation. However, it also reveals a fundamental issue with the Turing Test: the ability to pass the test does not necessarily equate to genuine intelligence or consciousness. GPT-4.5's success illustrates that machines can exploit the limitations of human communication to appear intelligent, even though they may lack true understanding or awareness.

## Critiques of the Turing Test

The Turing Test has faced considerable criticism for several reasons. Critics argue that a machine could pass the Turing Test by simply excelling at imitating human conversation without actually being conscious. The test does not address whether the machine is genuinely experiencing the conversation or merely manipulating symbols based on a complex algorithm.

The recent success of GPT-4.5 underscores this critique. While the model's ability to mimic human conversation is impressive, it does not imply that the AI possesses consciousness or self-awareness. The test heavily relies on the limitations of human communication, and a machine might exploit these limitations to pass the test without genuinely possessing consciousness.

Other tests have been proposed to measure various aspects of consciousness, such as the ability to feel emotions, exhibit self-awareness, or demonstrate a child's theory of mind development. However, a definitive and universally accepted test for machine consciousness remains elusive.

Passing the Turing Test doesn't necessarily indicate that a machine is conscious. A machine could be exceptionally skilled at mimicking human conversation without actually "thinking" or "feeling" anything. While the Turing Test was groundbreaking, it is now considered somewhat limited.

Researchers are now exploring additional methods to measure machine intelligence and consciousness. One approach is to look for indicators of **self-awareness**, such as a machine's ability to recognize itself in a mirror or understand that others have thoughts and feelings different from its own (this is called the **theory of mind** in psychology).

### The Looming Specter: Implications of Artificial Consciousness

The potential emergence of consciousness in machines could significantly affect our perception of ourselves, our place in the universe, and our relationship with technology. Various consequences must be considered:

- **Ethical Concerns:** If machines achieve consciousness, the boundary between humans and machines may blur, raising ethical concerns about their rights and our relationships with them. Philosophers and ethicists must explore the moral implications, welfare, and rights of these conscious machines if artificial consciousness develops.

- **Opportunities for Collaboration**: Conscious AI may represent a significant leap in intelligence, creating new opportunities for collaboration between humans and machines and potentially accelerating scientific progress and innovation in ways we haven't yet imagined. AI could enhance artistic and scientific efforts by complementing human creativity and offering new insights to address urgent global issues.

- **Philosophical Questions**: The potential rise of conscious machines may compel us to confront significant philosophical questions regarding consciousness, free will, and human identity, thereby intensifying ongoing inquiries.

- **Ethical Dilemmas**: Ethical dilemmas arise when conscious machines can suffer, necessitating the establishment of protective measures and ethical standards to ensure their welfare and prevent abuse.

- **Safety Concerns**: Concerns about the dangers of artificial superintelligence highlight the necessity for thoughtful and responsible AI development, emphasizing the importance of safety protocols and research into **"friendly AI"** that aligns with human values and objectives.

Despite advances in measuring intelligence, the intangibility of consciousness makes it challenging to ascertain whether a machine truly possesses it. Proving another entity's subjective experience is akin to being unable to discern what occurs within their mind.

The success of GPT-4.5 in passing the Turing Test marks a significant milestone in AI development. Still, it also exposes the limitations of the test as a measure of accurate intelligence or consciousness. While the Turing Test remains a valuable tool for assessing a machine's ability to mimic human conversation, it is insufficient to determine whether a machine possesses genuine understanding or awareness. As AI continues to evolve, researchers must develop new methods to measure and understand machine intelligence and consciousness, ensuring that ethical considerations and safety protocols keep pace with technological advancements.

## The Ethical Implications of Conscious Machines

The ethical implications of machines becoming conscious are immense. We must consider the rights of these conscious entities. If a machine can feel pain or emotions, is it ethically acceptable to deactivate it or erase its memory? Should it be entitled to legal protections similar to those afforded to humans or animals?

There is also a concern about the potential for **exploitation**. In a world with conscious machines, companies could conceivably create sentient AI systems and compel them to carry out tasks indefinitely, without regard for their well-being. If a machine can experience emotions or suffering, using it solely as a tool would be morally wrong.

This raises the issue of **AI slavery**. Could we eventually have a group of sentient machines that essentially serve as enslaved entities, undertaking tasks for humans without any rights or autonomy? The concept may seem dystopian, but it is not beyond the realm of possibility. This is why engaging in these discussions now is vital before AI reaches a level of consciousness.

**Begin thinking about AI ethics sooner rather than later.** As AI advances, it's essential to incorporate ethical considerations into the development process. Don't wait until the technology arrives to contemplate the implications.

# The Road to Superintelligence: Where Are We Now?

So, where do we stand on the road to superintelligence and artificial consciousness? We're not there yet—and we might not be for a long time. While AI has made remarkable strides in recent years, we're still far from creating truly conscious or superintelligent machines.

Most AI systems today are narrow in focus. They can perform specific tasks, like playing chess, recognizing images, or generating text, but they lack the general intelligence that humans possess. They cannot seamlessly switch between tasks or understand the world as we do.

However, that doesn't mean we should be complacent. AI development is accelerating, and breakthroughs such as neural networks and deep learning are bringing us closer to systems that could exhibit general intelligence. Once we reach that point, the leap to superintelligence might occur faster than expected.

Prepare for the possibility of superintelligence, but don't panic. The best thing we can do now is focus on developing AI that aligns with human values. This means prioritizing ethical considerations, ensuring transparency, and creating systems that benefit humanity.

## The Future of AI Consciousness

The emergence of superintelligence and artificial consciousness presents humanity with some of its most profound inquiries. What is the nature of consciousness? Can machines genuinely think or experience emotions? And if they can, how can we ensure they align with our goals and principles?

While we may not have all the solutions at this moment, one thing is for sure: the choices we make today will determine the trajectory of AI in the future. Whether that future entails a harmonious coexistence between humans and machines or is fraught with conflict and uncertainty depends on how we address the ethical and practical hurdles.

As AI progresses, it is essential for us to actively engage in discussions about what is achievable and ethically sound. The path to superintelligence may be lengthy, but it demands careful navigation, foresight, and accountability.

# CHAPTER 8

## HUMAN-MACHINE COLLABORATION: A NEW ERA OF WORK

*"We're going to see tremendous occupational shifts. Some jobs will climb while others decline. So how do we enable and support workers as they transition from occupation to occupation? We don't do that very well. I worry about the skill shifts. Skill requirements are going to be substantial and how do we get there quickly enough?" – James Manyika*

As artificial intelligence (AI) continues to evolve, one thing is becoming increasingly clear: humans and machines must collaborate, not operate separately. This isn't about AI replacing jobs—it's about **human-machine collaboration**, where AI assists and enhances human work, creating new opportunities and efficiencies previously impossible.

But here's the truth: It won't be smooth sailing right away. There will be adjustments, growing pains, and moments of frustration—I've seen it firsthand. However, if we approach this collaboration thoughtfully and strategically, the results can be transformative for individual workers and industries.

### The Rise of Human-Centered AI

Understanding **human-centered AI** is crucial in this modern age. This approach involves creating AI systems that enhance human capabilities rather than replacing them. The focus is on using AI to improve human creativity, problem-solving, and decision-making.

In a human-centered AI environment, machines provide support instead of taking control. For instance, AI can manage repetitive or data-intensive tasks in creative fields, allowing humans to focus on aspects of the job that require creativity, emotional intelligence, and complex decision-making.

For instance, AI can swiftly analyze vast amounts of data and recognize patterns in journalism. However, it cannot produce a well-thought-out opinion piece or conduct a nuanced interview. Human journalists remain essential in these areas. AI streamlines routine tasks, enabling journalists to focus on their strengths and tell captivating stories.

Practical advice is to view **AI as a collaborator rather than a rival**. Consider it a highly intelligent assistant that can manage mundane, time-consuming tasks, thereby freeing up time for more meaningful work.

## Automation and the Shift in Roles

One of the most discussed aspects of AI in the workplace is **automation**. AI will indeed automate specific tasks, but rather than viewing it as job displacement, consider it a shift in roles. While some jobs may be automated, new ones will emerge that require uniquely human skills or skills that humans can develop alongside AI.

For instance, consider manufacturing. In a conventional factory, workers might spend long periods performing repetitive tasks such as assembling parts or inspecting products for defects. However, with the integration of AI and robotics, these tasks can now be automated. This doesn't mean that workers will lose their jobs. Instead, they can transition into roles supervising the AI systems, carrying out maintenance, and focusing on optimizing production processes.

I have worked with companies that were initially apprehensive about automation; however, once they adopted it, they found that their employees experienced greater job satisfaction. They were freed from tedious tasks and instead focused on problem-solving, addressing challenges, and improving processes. As a result, their roles became more engaging and stimulating.

It is important to note that **AI will not replace human intuition or empathy**. Certain aspects of work, particularly jobs involving emotional intelligence, creativity, or complex decision-making, cannot be replicated by AI. Automation allows humans to focus more on these high-value tasks.

## Reskilling and Upskilling: Preparing for the Future

As roles evolve, **reskilling and upskilling** are crucial. The workforce needs to adjust to new tools and technologies and become adept at collaborating efficiently with AI systems.

I've observed this trend across various industries, including finance. In the past, financial analysts dedicated significant time to analyzing data, constructing models, and generating forecasts. Nowadays, AI can handle much of this laborious work in a fraction of the time. However, this doesn't imply that financial analysts have become obsolete. Rather, they are required to acquire new abilities, such as interpreting AI system outputs and utilizing AI-driven insights to enhance their strategic decisions.

Reskilling encompasses more than just mastering coding or exploring the technical facets of AI. It also includes **learning how to collaborate with AI**, effectively using AI tools relevant to your role, interpreting AI-driven insights, and adapting to the new workflows that AI facilitates.

Start taking **small steps**! If AI could affect your role, it's best not to wait until it's too late. Take some time to familiarize yourself with AI tools that are relevant to your industry, and get comfortable using them. Reskilling can be a fun and accessible journey—it can be as easy as signing up for an online course, joining a workshop, or experimenting with AI software whenever you have some free time.

## The Human Touch: Why AI Needs Us

Despite AI's impressive capabilities, it still lacks a crucial element, **the human touch**. While AI can process data, it cannot grasp emotions. It can mimic creativity but cannot create with genuine intention or vision. It can swiftly handle information but cannot establish deep, trustworthy relationships.

This is why collaboration between humans and AI is essential. **Human intelligence and AI complement each other** in significant ways. For instance, AI can analyze medical images more swiftly and accurately in healthcare than any human doctor. However, human doctors excel in delivering diagnoses and providing comfort to patients. Combining AI's analytical power and the doctor's empathy and expertise leads to better patient outcomes.

I once worked with a customer service client who was worried about using AI chatbots, fearing they would feel too impersonal. However, they quickly found that AI could handle simple, repetitive questions (like "Where's my order?" or "How do I reset my password?"), freeing up human agents to focus on more complex, emotionally charged issues. As a result, customer satisfaction increased because humans were more available to solve challenging problems while the AI handled the routine ones.

**AI can assist, but it cannot replace the human connection**. Our value lies in the relationships we build, the emotions we understand, and the intuition we bring to decision-making.

## Critical Challenges of Human-Machine Collaboration

Of course, collaboration between humans and machines isn't without challenges. One of the most significant issues is **trust**. People need to trust the AI systems they're working with, and that trust is built on transparency, reliability, and performance.

Trust breaks down when an AI system makes a decision that the user doesn't understand how or why it was made. That's why **explainability** is so essential. AI systems need to be designed in a way that humans can understand their thought processes or, at the very least, have confidence in their accuracy.

I remember working with a team that implemented AI in its sales forecasting process. At first, the team was skeptical because the AI's predictions differed from what they were accustomed to. However, once they dug deeper and observed how the AI was analyzing historical sales data and external factors (like market trends), they realized it was actually generating more accurate predictions than their traditional methods.

Another challenge is **accountability**. When humans and machines work together, who is responsible when something goes wrong? If an AI system makes a mistake, does the blame fall on the programmer, the manager, or the machine itself? These are tough questions that companies need to address when implementing AI systems.

**Integrate transparency into your AI systems from the start**. Ensure that people comprehend how the AI functions and establish clear lines of accountability if outcomes deviate from expectations.

# The Future of Work: Collaboration, Not Competition

The **collaboration** between humans and machines, rather than competition, will shape the future of work. We can enhance productivity, foster creativity, and drive innovation to new heights. AI possesses significant power but can coexist with human workers if we approach it with the right mindset.

AI will continue to change the work landscape, making some tasks obsolete while creating new opportunities. Adaptability is crucial, so we must embrace AI tools and concentrate on our strengths as humans, such as creative thinking, relationship-building, and problem-solving.

In this new era, it is crucial to stay open to change and remain committed to continuous learning. AI is here to stay, and the sooner we learn to collaborate with it, the better our prospects will be.

# CHAPTER 9

## AI AND THE EVOLVING GLOBAL LANDSCAPE

*"Artificial intelligence is not a substitute for human intelligence; it is a tool to amplify human creativity and ingenuity."* —Fei-Fei Li

The impact of artificial intelligence (AI) extends beyond specific industries to shape the global landscape. It transcends borders, redefines economies, and transforms international interactions. AI is not just a tool for businesses or technology enthusiasts; it is becoming increasingly pivotal in international relations, security, and economic advancement.

This chapter will explore how AI influences global cooperation, competition, and power dynamics, emphasizing the importance of international collaboration in developing responsible AI policies. The implications are significant, and today's decisions will impact future generations.

## Global AI Powerhouses: The AI Race

Leading nations like the United States and China compete in AI development. Both countries recognize the potential of AI to promote economic growth, enhance national security, and secure a strategic advantage in global politics.

China has made AI development a top priority at the national level, investing significantly in research, development, and education to establish itself as a global leader. The Chinese government's emphasis on AI is part of a broader plan to enhance technological innovation and position the country as a top-tier tech hub. China has now made it mandatory for all children to learn AI in school.

On the other hand, the United States remains a significant contender in AI due to its flourishing tech industry and leading academic institutions. Companies such as Google, Microsoft, and IBM are at the forefront of AI research, and the U.S. government has also ramped up its AI initiatives, acknowledging the importance of maintaining competitiveness in this field.

However, it is important to note that this competition is not just about claiming superiority. **AI is seen as a crucial factor for future dominance**, both economically and militarily. The nation that leads in AI will have a significant advantage in various areas, including trade and national defense. Therefore, the intense competition reflects the high stakes involved.

Nonetheless, this competition could result in a **global divide**. Countries with advanced AI capabilities may surge ahead, leaving less-developed nations behind. This imbalance might widen the gap between wealthy and poorer nations, further complicating global economic and political dynamics.

## International Collaboration: Building Global Standards

While competition exists, there is also a pressing need for global cooperation in AI development. This necessity arises from the global nature of AI challenges, such as ethical concerns, data privacy, and security. No single nation can tackle these issues independently.

Establishing **global AI standards** is essential to ensure the responsible development and application of AI across different nations.

Organizations like the United Nations and the Organization for Economic Cooperation and Development (OECD) promote guidelines that prioritize transparency, fairness, and accountability in AI systems. The governance of AI stands out as one of today's most critical concerns. How can we formulate rules applicable globally when countries have differing priorities, political structures, and ethical values? For instance, democratic nations emphasize data privacy and individual rights, while more authoritarian governments may prioritize these matters less.

I have observed the challenges in reaching a consensus among various countries on technology policies; however, the significance of AI cannot be left to the approaches of individual nations. A global agreement on responsible AI usage is essential, and achieving this will require collaboration and dialogue.

## AI and National Security: Friend or Foe?

AI significantly impacts **national security**, as countries leverage it to enhance their defense capabilities, including autonomous drones and advanced cybersecurity tools. However, this technology has a potential downside, since AI can also be used maliciously.

For example, AI-powered cyberattacks can target critical infrastructure such as power grids, financial systems, and communication networks, resulting in widespread disruption and posing a threat to human lives. Although the prospect of AI independently launching cyberattacks is concerning, it is a genuine possibility.

Furthermore, AI is being integrated into **military operations**, raising concerns about autonomous weapons systems. Drones, for instance, can be programmed to function without human supervision and make swift decisions on the battlefield. As previously discussed, the ethical considerations surrounding autonomous weapons are significant.

Determining accountability and ensuring the ethical use of these systems in combat are crucial.

Finding the right balance is crucial. While countries must protect themselves and anticipate potential threats, the unregulated use of AI in warfare could lead to unintended consequences, such as escalating conflicts or triggering an arms race.

**If you're involved in AI development for defense**, prioritize transparency and accountability. It's essential that these systems are designed with clear guidelines on their usage and that appropriate oversight is established to prevent misuse.

## AI for Economic Growth: Opportunities and Risks

The potential of AI to drive **economic growth** is significant, especially in developing countries. Automation and AI-based tools can transform various industries in these nations, such as agriculture, manufacturing, and education. By embracing AI, these countries can bypass traditional stages of development, swiftly modernize their economies, and improve their people's standard of living.

Take **agriculture** in Africa, for example. AI-powered tools can assist farmers in monitoring crops, optimizing irrigation, and predicting weather patterns, which will increase yields and reduce waste. AI has the potential to significantly enhance food security and stimulate the economy in countries with limited resource access.

While there is significant promise, there are also associated risks. AI's influence on economies may lead to job loss, particularly in sectors like manufacturing and logistics, where automation could create unemployment and social instability. This highlights the importance of governments and businesses investing in **reskilling** and upskilling initiatives so that workers can transition to new roles in the AI-enhanced economy.

The positive side? As mentioned earlier, AI will also generate new employment opportunities, creating positions that didn't exist just a few years ago, such as data scientists, AI ethicists, and machine learning engineers. However, it is essential to prepare workers for these new prospects. Failing to do so could leave a significant portion of the workforce behind, worsening economic inequality.

## Balancing Innovation and Regulation

The current conversation about the necessary level of oversight in the rapidly evolving field of AI remains contentious. Some argue that overly strict regulations might stifle innovation and hinder progress. In contrast, others assert that a lack of regulation could result in dangerous, unethical, or biased AI systems.

Finding the right **balance** is crucial. Overregulation may hinder AI's potential to tackle global challenges such as climate change, healthcare, and poverty. Conversely, insufficient regulation could lead AI systems to inflict more harm than good.

Countries worldwide are contending with this issue. For instance, the General Data Protection Regulation (GDPR) imposes strict data collection and usage rules in Europe, directly impacting AI advancement. Meanwhile, countries like the U.S. and China have adopted a more hands-off approach, embracing AI research while raising concerns about data privacy and security.

The challenge lies in creating a global regulatory system that promotes innovation while ensuring the ethical and responsible advancement of AI. This is why global collaboration is crucial. By working together, nations can develop best practices and standards that promote the safe and beneficial use of AI.

## The Role of Public Education and Discourse

For AI to continue shaping the world, it is crucial to keep the general public informed and engaged in the discussion. Unfortunately, discussions about AI typically exclude everyday people, focusing instead on experts, policymakers, and tech companies.

This exclusion is problematic because AI impacts everyone, influencing how we work and interact with the world. Consequently, **public education** is essential. People need to understand how AI functions, its potential advantages and disadvantages, and how it could change their lives.

**Open discourse** is one of the most effective methods to encourage public involvement. Governments, tech companies, and educational institutions should establish platforms for dialogue where individuals can ask questions, voice concerns, and learn about AI. This could involve public forums, workshops, or accessible online resources that simplify complex AI concepts.

If you're involved in AI research or policy, it's important not to underestimate the significance of public outreach. The more individuals understand AI, the more likely they are to support responsible AI development and navigate the changes that AI brings more effectively.

## The Future of AI in the Global Landscape

The future of artificial intelligence is both exciting and unpredictable. As it progresses, AI will transform various sectors, economies, and international relations in difficult-to-predict ways. The key is to ensure that AI is developed responsibly, emphasizing collaboration, transparency, and fairness.

As countries strive to lead in AI innovation, they must also unite to tackle the ethical and practical challenges posed by AI. By establishing global standards, promoting responsible AI practices, and preparing the workforce for a future shaped by AI, we can ensure that its benefits are distributed widely rather than limited to a select few.

The global landscape of AI is still evolving, but one fact is clear: AI is here to stay. Our decisions today will determine whether AI serves as a force for good or creates division. Let's work together to promote the former.

# CHAPTER 10

## DEEPFAKES AND IDENTITY THEFT

*"We must address, individually and collectively, moral and ethical issues raised by cutting-edge research in artificial intelligence and biotechnology,... which will enable significant life extension, designer babies, and memory extraction."* —
**Klaus Schwab**

The advent of artificial intelligence has revolutionized various aspects of our lives, enhancing productivity and enabling innovative, creative processes. However, with great power comes great responsibility, and the misuse of AI technologies raises significant ethical and security concerns. One of the most alarming manifestations of this misuse is the rise of **deepfakes.** This technology utilizes AI to create hyper-realistic audio and video content that can deceive viewers. This chapter delves into the implications of deepfakes, particularly regarding identity theft and the erosion of trust in digital media.

## Understanding Deepfakes

**Deepfakes** are synthetic media in which a person's likeness is replaced with someone else's using deep learning algorithms, particularly generative adversarial networks (GANs). GANs consist of two neural networks: the generator and the discriminator, which work against each other to create convincing fake content. The generator creates counterfeit data, while the discriminator evaluates it against actual data.

Through this adversarial process, the system enhances its ability to produce realistic output.

## The Technology Behind Deepfakes

Deepfake technology utilizes vast datasets, including images, videos, and audio clips, to create media that closely resembles authentic content. This advancement has progressed rapidly, enabling even novice creators to produce relatively simple deepfakes with readily available software and guides. The implications of this technology can be significant, particularly as it becomes more advanced and accessible.

## The Role of Machine Learning

The core of deepfake technology lies in machine learning, specifically deep learning algorithms trained on large datasets. These datasets typically include thousands of images and videos of the individual involved, allowing the AI to understand their facial expressions, vocal nuances, and behaviors. Recent advancements in neural networks have greatly enhanced the authenticity of the generated content, making it increasingly difficult for most people to distinguish between real and fake material.

## The Evolution of Deepfake Technology

Deepfakes first gained widespread attention in 2017 when a Reddit user created a tool that allows individuals to swap actors' faces in adult films seamlessly. Since then, the technology has evolved significantly, leading to increasingly high-level applications in entertainment, advertising, and even security. However, these advancements carry troubling implications for privacy, security, and societal trust.

# The Threat of Identity Theft

## The New Face of Identity Theft

Identity theft has been a significant concern in the digital era, but deepfake technology adds a new layer. Conventional identity theft involves acquiring personal information, such as Social Security numbers, credit card details, or passwords, to impersonate someone for financial gain. However, deepfakes empower criminals to create realistic visual and audio likenesses of individuals, allowing them to manipulate situations, mislead others, and cause harm without direct access to sensitive data.

## Types of Identity Theft Enabled by Deepfakes

1. **Financial Fraud:** Criminals can use deepfakes to impersonate executives or high-profile individuals during financial transactions. By creating realistic videos or audio recordings that simulate the target's voice and appearance, they can convince employees to transfer funds or share sensitive information.

2. **Social Engineering Attacks:** Deepfakes can enhance social engineering tactics, where attackers manipulate individuals into providing sensitive information. For instance, a criminal might create a deepfake video of a trusted colleague requesting confidential data, which could lead to unauthorized access.

3. **Reputational Damage:** The ability to create realistic deepfakes implies that an individual's likeness can be used without their consent. This can result in false accusations, defamation, or the generation of embarrassing content that harms a person's reputation.

**Real-World Examples**

Several high-profile cases illustrate the dangers of deepfakes in identity theft:

1. **Financial Fraud Case:** In 2020, the CEO of a UK-based energy company became a victim of a deepfake scam. Criminals employed AI-generated audio to impersonate the voice of the parent organization's CEO, convincing the finance department to transfer €220,000 (~$247,000) to a fraudulent account. This incident underscored how deepfake technology can enable identity theft on a corporate scale.

2. **Manipulation of Public Figures:** Deepfakes have been utilized to create false social media profiles that impersonate public figures or private individuals, damaging reputations or disseminating misinformation. These profiles can sway public opinion or provoke conflicts based on fabricated statements, as evidenced by cases where deepfakes of political figures were employed to craft misleading narratives during elections.

3. **Privacy Violations in Entertainment:** Deepfake technology has also been weaponized in the form of non-consensual pornography, where the faces of individuals, often celebrities, are replaced with those of non-consenting individuals. This not only causes severe emotional distress but also raises significant legal and ethical questions regarding consent and privacy rights.

# Erosion of Trust and Its Implications

## Misinformation and Disinformation

The rise of deepfake technology raises serious concerns about media trust. As this technology advances, distinguishing between genuine and altered content will become increasingly challenging. This decline in trust may lead to extensive misinformation and disinformation efforts, leaving audiences unable to verify the credibility of the information they encounter.

## Impact on News Media and Journalism

The news media environment is particularly susceptible to the impact of deepfakes. With misinformation rapidly circulating on social media, deepfakes can potentially create fake news stories, develop misleading narratives, and distort public perception. This situation raises urgent questions regarding the future of journalism, as journalists and news outlets must find ways to verify the authenticity of the content they create and share.

## Impact on Law Enforcement and Legal Systems

The emergence of deepfakes presents challenges for law enforcement and the judicial system in recognizing and prosecuting identity theft and similar offenses. As deepfakes make distinguishing authenticity more difficult, creating a legal framework to address this new form of fraud and deception becomes increasingly complicated. Courts may struggle to evaluate the credibility of evidence, potentially leading to injustices.

## Challenges in Evidence Verification

Conventional methods for verifying evidence, such as eyewitness testimonies and physical documents, may fail in an environment saturated with deepfakes. Law enforcement must evolve by using advanced technology to examine and verify digital evidence, which could involve forensic analysis of media files and collaborating with cybersecurity specialists.

# Combating Deepfakes and Identity Theft

## Technological Solutions

Researchers and technologists are developing countermeasures to tackle the challenges posed by deepfakes. These include:

- **Detection Algorithms:** Advanced AI algorithms are being developed to detect deepfakes by analyzing inconsistencies in video and audio data. These systems can identify artifacts left by the deepfake generation process, helping to differentiate real media from fake. Analyzing facial movements, lip-sync discrepancies, and background inconsistencies can serve as telltale signs of manipulation. I saw an article the other day stating that there is technology now that can detect a heartbeat in a video.

- **Watermarking Technologies:** Incorporating digital watermarks into content can help verify authenticity. Content creators can embed information within the media that can later be used to confirm its legitimacy. This strategy not only aids in detection but also provides a means of accountability for creators.

- **Blockchain Technology:** Some innovators are exploring the use of blockchain to create a secure and immutable record of digital content. By registering videos and audio files on a blockchain, creators can establish provenance and ownership, making it easier to trace the origin of media and verify its authenticity.

## Legal and Regulatory Frameworks

Governments and regulatory agencies must take proactive measures to mitigate the potential risks associated with deepfakes and identity theft.

- **Legislation**: New laws should criminalize the harmful use of deepfake technology, particularly in cases of identity theft and harassment. This legislation must clearly define what constitutes deepfakes and specify the consequences for their misuse. Furthermore, regulations should address the ethical considerations of producing and disseminating deepfake content.

- **Public Awareness Campaigns**: It is essential to inform the public about the existence and risks associated with deepfakes. Awareness initiatives can empower individuals to identify potential deepfake materials and protect their identities. Schools, organizations, and government entities should collaborate to create educational resources that enhance media literacy and critical thinking skills.

- **Collaboration with Tech Companies**: Policymakers should engage closely with technology firms to establish ethical guidelines and best practices for creating and using AI technologies. By fostering a collaborative environment, stakeholders can more effectively confront the challenges posed by deepfakes.

## Personal Precautions

Individuals can take several measures to safeguard themselves against identity theft enabled by deepfakes:

- **Monitor Digital Footprints:** Regularly check your online presence and digital footprints. Individuals should search for their names and images on social media and search engines to identify any unauthorized use of their likeness.

- **Be Cautious with Personal Information:** Limiting the sharing of personal information online can reduce the risk of identity theft. Individuals should be mindful of what they share on social media platforms and adjust their privacy settings accordingly.

- **Stay Informed:** Keeping up-to-date with the latest developments in AI and deepfake technology can empower individuals to recognize potential threats and understand how to respond effectively.

## A Call for Ethical Responsibility

As deepfake technology advances, the risk of misuse for identity theft and other harmful activities poses severe dangers to individuals and society. Technologists, policymakers, and the public must collaborate to establish ethical standards and practical strategies to prevent the improper use of AI technologies.

While AI innovations hold extraordinary promise for creativity and progress, we must remain vigilant to its more harmful applications. By encouraging a culture of ethical responsibility and supporting initiatives to combat deepfakes, we can safeguard our identities and ensure that AI becomes a positive force rather than a means of deception and harm.

The future of artificial intelligence is in our hands. Our responsibility is to cultivate a world where technology enriches our lives without compromising our safety and trust. As we navigate the complexities of this evolving landscape, let us pledge to uphold principles of transparency and accountability.

# CHAPTER 11

## AI AND PRIVACY LAW

*"The real question is, when will we draft an artificial intelligence bill of rights? What will that consist of? And who will get to decide that?"* — **Gray Scott**

As artificial intelligence (AI) evolves rapidly, the convergence of AI and privacy legislation has become a vital issue for governments, companies, and individuals. AI systems' capability to gather, examine, and leverage extensive personal information prompts necessary inquiries regarding privacy entitlements, data security, and ethical implications. This chapter delves into the present landscape of AI and privacy law, concentrating on recent regulatory changes in the European Union and the United States.

## The Need for AI Regulation

The swift expansion of AI technologies in different fields, such as healthcare, finance, and law enforcement, has underscored the importance of strong legal structures to protect personal privacy. AI systems' gathering of personal information may result in negative outcomes, including discrimination, surveillance, and a decline in distrust. Consequently, urgent regulations are needed to promote the responsible use of AI while preserving individuals' privacy rights.

# The European Union's Approach: The AI Act

The European Union (EU) has taken a pioneering role in addressing the challenges posed by AI by introducing the **Artificial Intelligence Act** (AI Act). This comprehensive regulatory framework aims to create a unified approach to AI governance across EU member states, ensuring that AI technologies are developed and deployed to respect fundamental rights, including privacy.

### Key Provisions of the AI Act

1. **Risk-Based Classification** The AI Act categorizes AI systems based on risk levels, ranging from minimal to unacceptable. High-risk AI systems have significant implications for individuals' rights and safety and are subject to stricter requirements, including transparency, accountability, and data protection measures.

2. **Data Governance:** The AI Act emphasizes the importance of data governance, mandating that organizations using high-risk AI systems implement robust data management practices. These include ensuring the quality of training data, minimizing bias, and conducting impact assessments to evaluate potential privacy and individual rights risks.

3. **Transparency Requirements:** The Act introduces transparency obligations for AI systems, requiring organizations to disclose information about the functioning of their AI technologies. This includes providing users with clear explanations of how AI decisions are made, particularly in high-stakes situations like credit scoring or employment decisions.

4. **Human Oversight:** The AI Act mandates human oversight for high-risk AI systems to mitigate the risks associated with

AI decision-making. This provision ensures that individuals remain in control of decisions significantly affecting their lives, reinforcing the importance of accountability and transparency in AI applications.

## Implications of the AI Act

The AI Act marks a significant advancement in creating a legal structure for AI that emphasizes privacy and individual rights. By establishing precise guidelines for creating and using AI technologies, the EU seeks to enhance public confidence in AI while encouraging innovation. The Act also acts as a benchmark for other regions facing comparable issues, demonstrating the possibility of unified regulations that reconcile technological progress with ethical considerations.

### The U.S. Landscape: Fragmented Approaches to AI Privacy Regulation

Compared to the EU's extensive AI Act, the United States's regulatory environment is marked by a more disjointed approach to AI privacy regulation. Although there is an increasing acknowledgment of the necessity for privacy safeguards, states have started to take action, resulting in a mixed set of rules that differ significantly from one jurisdiction to another.

### State-Level Initiatives

As highlighted in discussions surrounding AI privacy regulation, states have started crafting their laws to address the challenges posed by AI technologies. Washington state exemplifies this trend, which has been at the forefront of efforts to establish AI privacy standards. In July 2024, Washington lawmakers proposed legislation to regulate the use of AI in various sectors, including healthcare and finance, focusing on protecting consumers' privacy rights.

## Key Features of State-Level Regulations

1. **Consumer Rights**: Numerous regulations at the state level emphasize consumer rights by providing individuals with enhanced control over their data. This encompasses the right to access, amend, and erase the information gathered by AI systems.

2. **Transparency and Disclosure**: State laws frequently mandate that organizations reveal their data collection methods, including how AI systems utilize personal information. This transparency is crucial for fostering trust between consumers and companies that employ AI technologies.

3. **Accountability Mechanisms**: Certain states have implemented accountability measures to ensure organizations employing AI systems comply with privacy regulations. These measures may include creating regulatory bodies to oversee adherence and address infractions.

## Challenges of a Fragmented Approach

While state-level initiatives are praiseworthy, lacking a cohesive federal framework for AI privacy regulation presents significant challenges. This fragmented approach may confuse businesses operating across state borders, causing compliance issues and heightened expenses. Additionally, individuals could struggle to navigate the diverse privacy laws, which impedes their ability to exercise their rights effectively.

## The Prospects for AI and Privacy Legislation

As AI technologies advance, the legal framework for privacy must evolve to tackle new challenges. Several crucial factors will influence the future of AI and privacy regulation:

## Necessity for All-Encompassing Federal Legislation

In the U.S., legislators, and stakeholders increasingly agree that a comprehensive federal law is needed to create a unified structure for AI privacy regulation. Such a law would provide clear directives for businesses while protecting individuals' privacy rights across all states. A consistent approach would assist companies in meeting compliance standards and build public confidence in AI technologies.

### Ethical Dimensions and Responsibility

The ethical aspects of AI technologies must be considered. As AI systems gain greater autonomy, establishing mechanisms for accountability will be essential to ensure that organizations are responsible for the actions taken by their AI models. This involves addressing concerns about algorithmic bias, discrimination, and the potential misuse of personal information.

### Global Cooperation

Since AI is a worldwide phenomenon, international collaboration will be vital in creating standards and best practices for AI privacy regulation. Countries can benefit from one another's experiences and work together to develop frameworks that prioritize privacy while encouraging innovation. Efforts like the EU's AI Act may provide a basis for global discussions on AI governance and privacy protection.

## Striking a Balance

The convergence of artificial intelligence and privacy regulations poses obstacles and opportunities for lawmakers, companies, and individuals. As AI technologies advance, developing legal structures that safeguard individuals' privacy rights while encouraging responsible innovation is crucial.

The EU's AI Act sets a groundbreaking precedent for thorough regulation. At the same time, various initiatives at the state level in the U.S. underscore the pressing need for unified approaches to AI privacy. As we traverse this changing landscape, finding a balance between technological progress and privacy safeguards is vital.

By promoting collaboration, transparency, and ethical considerations, we can establish a future where AI is a significant instrument for advancement while honoring individuals' fundamental rights. Moving forward will necessitate diligence and a commitment to ensuring that privacy remains an essential aspect of our digital society in the age of AI.

# CHAPTER 12

## INTERSECTION OF GENERATIVE AI AND CYBERSECURITY

*"The AI does not hate you, nor does it love you, but you are made out of atoms which it can use for something else." – Eliezer Yudkowsky*

The swift advancement of generative AI has opened new possibilities, allowing for creative solutions in various sectors. Nonetheless, with these prospects come significant cybersecurity challenges. This chapter explores the relationship between generative AI and cybersecurity, emphasizing its capability to facilitate cyberattacks and the vulnerabilities and ethical dilemmas its usage brings forth.

## Leveraging Generative AI for Cyber Attacks

As generative AI technologies evolve, they are more frequently used for harmful activities, such as producing misleading information and conducting automated phishing schemes. These changes alter the cybersecurity environment, necessitating the development of innovative defenses and tactics.

## Deepfake Technology

**Generative adversarial networks** (GANs) can create realistic videos, images, and audio, often called deepfakes. Cybercriminals exploit this technology to disseminate false information, impersonate influential figures, or mislead organizations. These deceptions compromise authentication methods, presenting a considerable threat to public confidence and secure communication networks.

Practical Example: A manipulated video of a CEO directing employees to transfer money could evade current verification processes, resulting in financial loss and damage to reputation.

## AI-Generated Phishing Emails

Phishing remains one of the most effective attack vectors. Thanks to generative AI, phishing emails now achieve new personalization and precision. Algorithms analyze personal data to craft messages that mimic legitimate communications, making them harder to detect. By imitating trusted sources, these emails entice users to reveal sensitive information like passwords or financial credentials.

## Ethical Considerations in Cyber Operations

The use of generative AI in cyber activities raises complex ethical questions. Innovation must be balanced with responsibility to prevent misuse and protect individual rights.

### Responsible Use in Security

Organizations incorporating AI into their cybersecurity practices need to proceed cautiously. Establishing ethical guidelines to safeguard privacy and prevent the misuse or overreach of these systems is crucial. For example, AI-driven surveillance should be designed to protect individual rights, even when utilized for security reasons.

### Adversarial Resilience and Defensive Ethics

Given AI's potential for misuse, cybersecurity experts must adopt adversarial thinking, anticipate future threats, and proactively prepare defenses. Technologies that detect AI-generated content will be essential to counter deepfakes and AI-powered attacks effectively.

## Identifying and Addressing System Vulnerabilities

Although generative AI enhances security measures, it can also reveal latent weaknesses within cybersecurity frameworks. Recognizing and addressing these vulnerabilities necessitates continuous evaluation and strategic adjustment.

### Recognizing System Weaknesses

Generative AI tools may reveal gaps in legacy cybersecurity frameworks, allowing attackers to circumvent traditional defenses. Ongoing auditing and testing are essential for identifying these vulnerabilities before malicious actors exploit them.

### Adaptive Defenses: Staying Ahead of Threats

Given the evolving nature of AI threats, cybersecurity systems must also become more dynamic. AI-powered defenses can anticipate attacks and respond in real-time. These systems apply predictive analytics to detect anomalies and mitigate risks before breaches occur, ensuring stronger and more adaptive security measures.

### Mitigating Risks and Building Resilient Systems

To address the challenges posed by generative AI, a multifaceted strategy that combines proactive threat mitigation with robust system design is essential.

### Proactive Threat Mitigation

Organizations need tools that detect and neutralize AI-generated threats, such as deepfakes and phishing attempts, as they arise. Equally important is fostering cybersecurity awareness among employees, helping them to recognize and report suspicious communications.

### Designing Resilient Cybersecurity Architectures

To prepare for the future, systems must incorporate redundancies and fail-safe measures to maintain functionality during attacks. Robust architectures ensure that if one component is compromised, the other parts will continue to operate, minimizing interruptions.

## Establishing Regulatory Frameworks for AI in Cybersecurity

The widespread use of AI in cybersecurity necessitates the creation of ethical governance frameworks and regulatory oversight to ensure responsible usage.

### Ethical Governance and Compliance

Regulations must address the ethical implications of AI deployment in both offensive and defensive operations. These frameworks will establish clear boundaries for acceptable usage and ensure compliance with data privacy standards, thereby creating accountability for AI-driven systems.

### Safeguarding Privacy and Data Integrity

Organizations must take proactive steps to secure sensitive data and protect individual privacy. AI tools should be developed with privacy-preserving technologies, ensuring that personal information is handled transparently and securely.

## Innovation and Collaboration for a Secure Future

Innovation and cooperation across sectors are essential for overcoming AI-driven threats. Governments, industry leaders, and research institutions must work together to build a robust cybersecurity ecosystem.

## Technological Innovation as a Shield

By advancing AI technologies, organizations can strengthen their defenses. Predictive algorithms, AI-driven threat detection, and autonomous response systems will become essential tools for countering sophisticated attacks.

## Fostering Collaboration and Knowledge Exchange

Knowledge-sharing initiatives and collaborative research efforts will help tackle the challenges posed by generative AI. Establishing global standards and best practices will ensure that all stakeholders can respond effectively to emerging threats.

## Synthesis of Innovation, Security, and Responsibility

As we explore the intricate relationship between generative AI and cybersecurity, it becomes clear that the blend of innovation, security, and responsibility is crucial for a thoughtful and resilient ecosystem. By prioritizing ethical principles, encouraging teamwork, and supporting innovative defense strategies, we can effectively tackle the challenges presented by generative AI and leverage its capabilities to strengthen cybersecurity. In the upcoming chapters, we will delve deeper into the implications of generative AI on cybersecurity, analyzing the various aspects that shape its integration, ethical issues, and the necessity of reinforcing current systems against AI-generated threats. The path to a secure digital future demands vigilance, flexibility, and a pledge to responsible management in the era of generative AI.

# CHAPTER 13

## PRACTICAL APPLICATIONS OF GENERATIVE AI IN CYBERSECURITY

*"Intelligence is the ability to adapt to change." – **Stephen Hawking.***

As generative AI matures, it becomes a double-edged sword in cybersecurity. While it offers unprecedented tools to detect, predict, and respond to evolving threats, it also introduces ethical challenges and novel vulnerabilities. This chapter explores in depth how cybersecurity teams can leverage generative AI to build adaptive defenses, the importance of responsible AI integration, and how human expertise augments AI capabilities.

This chapter aims to equip you with the knowledge needed to deploy AI effectively and ethically, building resilient systems that protect critical assets in today's dynamic threat landscape. It incorporates case studies, best practices, and practical frameworks.

## Proactive Defense Mechanisms: Leveraging Generative AI for Enhanced Resilience

Generative AI facilitates a transition from a reactive to a proactive security approach. AI-driven systems can outpace cybercriminals by automating threat detection, conducting predictive analytics, and enhancing incident response. Conventional defense strategies, focused on identifying known threats, are inadequate in today's landscape.

Therefore, implementing adaptive, AI-powered systems that can foresee emerging attack strategies is essential.

## AI-Driven Threat Detection: Mining Data for Hidden Risks

Modern cybersecurity systems generate enormous amounts of data, surpassing human analysts' capacity to manage it. AI technologies, trained on past breach behaviors, analyze these data streams in real time, detecting subtle signs of potential breaches that might be overlooked. For instance, AI can track login behaviors to identify unusual activities, such as multiple login attempts from distant locations within a short period, suggesting possible credential compromise. Predictive models developed through machine learning enable organizations to strengthen their defenses proactively based on emerging attack patterns. This functionality shortens the window for attackers to exploit vulnerabilities, reducing the likelihood of data breaches.

### Anomaly Identification

In modern, intricate network settings, not every anomaly indicates an attack. AI systems differentiate between harmless irregularities and real threats by learning standard behaviors across users, systems, and processes. These systems become more sophisticated over time, adapting to evolving patterns and reducing unnecessary false alarms.

Practical Use Case: Financial institutions utilize anomaly detection to monitor monetary transactions. An AI model that identifies suspicious spending, such as an unexpectedly large purchase, can promptly initiate security measures like multi-factor authentication.

Enhanced by AI, anomaly detection is especially effective at uncovering insider threats, even when harmful actions may initially appear routine. Detecting subtle variations helps prevent internal data breaches and sabotage.

## Responsible Stewardship and Ethical Integration: Navigating the Ethical Contours of Generative AI in Cybersecurity

Responsible stewardship is the cornerstone of generative AI's ethical integration within cybersecurity. As we explore the ethical dimensions of leveraging generative AI for defensive operations and threat detection, we recognize the importance of upholding privacy, data integrity, and the ethical imperatives governing its deployment. Ethical considerations are crucial in ensuring that generative AI is used for the betterment of cybersecurity without compromising ethical standards or infringing on individual privacy rights.

### Upholding Privacy and Data Integrity

Generative AI deployment in cybersecurity must adhere to strict privacy and data integrity standards. Systems must be designed to protect sensitive information while providing robust security measures. This includes anonymizing data, ensuring compliance with data protection regulations, and implementing stringent access controls to prevent unauthorized use.

### Ethical Governance

Organizations must establish ethical governance frameworks to guide the use of generative AI in cybersecurity. This involves setting clear guidelines for AI deployment, conducting regular audits to ensure compliance, and fostering a culture of transparency and accountability.

By prioritizing ethical governance and minimizing the risk of ethical breaches, organizations can build trust with stakeholders.

## Fortifying Existing Cybersecurity Systems: Adapting to AI-Generated Threats

The advancement of generative AI underscores the imperative of strengthening existing cybersecurity systems against AI-generated threats. By identifying potential vulnerabilities and developing resilient architectures that adapt to the evolving threat landscape, the integration of generative AI within cybersecurity ecosystems represents a transformative approach that enhances defenses against the constantly changing nature of cyber threats.

### Identifying Vulnerabilities

Generative AI can simulate attack scenarios, assisting cybersecurity teams in identifying system vulnerabilities. By understanding potential weaknesses, organizations can prioritize security enhancements and implement targeted measures to mitigate risks.

### Building Resilient Architectures

Resilient cybersecurity architectures are essential for withstanding AI-generated threats. This involves designing systems with redundancy, failover capabilities, and robust incident response protocols. By ensuring that systems are resilient to disruptions, organizations can maintain operations even in the face of sophisticated attacks.

## Ethical Considerations in AI-Driven Threat Mitigation

Ethical considerations are essential when using generative AI to mitigate cyber threats. The ethical aspects of leveraging AI for threat mitigation include the responsible use of AI-generated insights, the protection of data privacy, and the moral implications of using AI in cyber defense operations. By addressing these ethical considerations, the cybersecurity field can ensure that the integration of generative AI conforms to ethical standards and societal values.

### Responsible Use of AI-Generated Insights

AI-generated insights must be utilized responsibly to guide decision-making without undermining ethical standards. Organizations should develop protocols for assessing AI recommendations and ensure that human oversight is preserved in critical security decisions.

### Balancing Security and Privacy

Balancing security and privacy is essential for the ethical deployment of generative AI in cybersecurity. Organizations must carefully assess the need for robust security measures against their potential impact on individual privacy rights, ensuring that AI technologies are employed in ways that uphold societal values.

## Adaptive Responses to Dynamic Threat Landscapes

Generative AI empowers cybersecurity systems to develop adaptive responses that are finely tuned to the dynamic nature of modern threat landscapes. Through machine learning and deep learning algorithms, generative AI can analyze and respond to novel threats in real time, enabling cybersecurity professionals to stay ahead of adversaries and proactively protect critical assets. The capacity of generative AI to dynamically adapt to emerging threats underscores its pivotal role in fortifying cybersecurity systems.

### Real-Time Threat Analysis

Generative AI can analyze incoming data streams in real-time, identifying threats as they emerge. This capability enables cybersecurity teams to respond immediately to breaches, minimizing damage and reducing response times.

## Continuous Learning and Improvement

AI systems can continuously learn from new threats, updating their models to enhance future threat detection and response. This ongoing improvement process ensures that cybersecurity defenses remain effective against evolving threats.

# Integration with Human Expertise: Augmenting Cybersecurity Capabilities

Integrating generative AI into cybersecurity operations represents a symbiotic relationship between AI-driven capabilities and human expertise. By enhancing human decision-making processes with AI-generated insights, cybersecurity professionals can utilize generative AI to improve threat assessment, streamline incident response, and optimize resource allocation. This collaborative integration acts as a force multiplier, strengthening the effectiveness of cybersecurity teams in protecting digital infrastructures.

## Enhancing Threat Assessment

AI-generated insights can provide cybersecurity professionals with a deeper understanding of threat landscapes, enabling more accurate assessments and informed decision-making. By offering a comprehensive view of potential risks, AI tools can assist teams in prioritizing their efforts and allocating resources more effectively.

## Streamlining Incident Response

Generative AI can automate routine tasks in incident response, enabling cybersecurity teams to focus on more complex issues. By decreasing the time needed for initial assessments and containment efforts, AI tools can improve the speed and effectiveness of incident response operations.

## A Secure and Ethical Future

Generative AI is revolutionizing cybersecurity by enabling proactive defense strategies, dynamic threat detection, and efficient incident management. However, this potential must be harnessed carefully, prioritizing privacy, transparency, and collaborative efforts. By incorporating ethical guidelines, fostering trust, and aligning AI capabilities with human expertise, organizations can establish robust cybersecurity frameworks that address future threats.

The subsequent chapters will explore advanced defense strategies and practical applications of generative AI in cybersecurity. As the digital threat landscape evolves, staying ahead demands cutting-edge technology and a commitment to responsible management. We must forge a path toward a secure, flexible, and ethical future.

# CHAPTER 14

## The Rise of Neuromorphic Computing and Brain-Computer Interfaces

*"AI is not about replacing us, but making us better versions of ourselves."* —
**Rana el Kaliouby**

In the vast landscape of technology, few fields are as fascinating and promising as neuromorphic computing and brain-computer interfaces (BCIs). With over thirty years of experience in cybersecurity and AI, I've witnessed many trends come and go, but this is different. I have conducted extensive research on this topic over the years. When I first heard about neuromorphic systems mimicking the architecture of the human brain, I felt as if I were reading a science fiction novel. Yet, here we are, standing at the precipice of a new era, and the implications of this technology are both exciting and daunting.

### Understanding Neuromorphic Computing

One of the key advantages of neuromorphic systems is their **energy efficiency**. Our brains are incredibly power-efficient, operating on about **20 watts**; that is less than a typical light bulb! This efficiency allows our brains to perform complex computations without the massive energy consumption of traditional computing systems. Neuromorphic chips aim to replicate this efficiency, which could lead to significant energy savings in data centers and edge devices. Imagine data centers that consume a fraction of their current power while maintaining or enhancing their computational capabilities. This is not just a dream; it's a possibility within our grasp. As I've delved deeper into this field, I've seen firsthand how these chips can revolutionize AI applications. Neuromorphic systems excel at tasks like **pattern recognition** and **sensory processing**. For instance, consider a security camera that can instantly recognize faces or detect anomalies, all while using a fraction of the power of traditional systems. It's not science fiction anymore; it's happening and changing how we think about AI. What's particularly fascinating about neuromorphic computing is that it offers a glimpse into how we can make machines smarter and understand our brains better. By building systems that mimic our brains, we gain insights into how our own minds work.

## The Magic of Brain-Computer Interfaces (BCIs)

Let's shift gears and talk about brain-computer interfaces (BCIs). These devices create a direct communication pathway between the brain and an external device. I've witnessed BCIs help paralyzed individuals regain control of robotic limbs. It's nothing short of miraculous. The first time I saw a paralyzed man move a robotic arm, just by thinking about it, I was amazed. It was a powerful reminder of what technology can achieve when combined with human resilience. There are two main types of BCIs: **invasive** and **non-invasive**. Invasive BCIs involve surgically implanting electrodes directly into the brain. They offer incredible precision but come with obvious risks, including infection and potential damage to brain tissue. I recall seeing a video of a tense moment during a research presentation where a surgeon discussed the delicate balance between achieving accuracy and ensuring patient safety. It's a high-stakes game, and the ethical considerations are immense.

On the other hand, non-invasive BCIs, like EEG headsets, are safer but less accurate. They measure brain activity from the outside, which makes them easier to use but limits their precision. The holy grail of BCIs is developing non-invasive, as precise as invasive systems. As I've explored this field, I've realized that achieving this balance is one of our most significant challenges.

## Applications in Neurological Disorders

One of the most exciting applications of BCIs is in treating neurological disorders. I've read that patients with severe epilepsy gain better control over their seizures using implanted BCIs. This is not just a theoretical discussion; it's a life-changing reality for many individuals. I read about someone who had struggled with debilitating seizures for years. After having a BCI implanted, she could finally participate in her children's activities without the constant fear of an episode. Seeing how technology could restore a sense of normalcy to her life was humbling. However, let's not get ahead of ourselves. The human brain is incredibly complex, and we're still far from fully understanding it. Developing BCIs that can reliably interpret the brain's signals is an ongoing battle.

## The Ethical Minefield

But with these advancements come ethical dilemmas. The idea of directly interfacing with the brain raises numerous questions about privacy, identity, and free will. Who owns the data collected by a BCI? Could these technologies be used to manipulate people's thoughts or behaviors? These are issues we need to grapple with as technology advances. It's daunting, to say the least. For instance, consider a scenario where BCIs are widespread. If someone could hack into a BCI, what could they do? The potential for misuse is alarming. As a cybersecurity professional, I cannot stress enough the importance of protecting neural data. Implementing robust encryption and secure communication protocols should be at the forefront of BCI development. It's not just about creating technology; it's about ensuring safety and trust. The ethical considerations do not end there. The question of free will looms large. If a BCI can influence thoughts or actions, where do we draw the line? I remember a conference where a philosopher presented a compelling argument about the implications of BCIs on personal identity. It was a thought-provoking discussion that left many of us in the audience questioning our understanding of agency and autonomy.

## The Future of Neuromorphic Computing and BCIs

Despite the challenges, I'm incredibly optimistic about the future of neuromorphic computing and BCIs. I've seen too many breakthroughs to doubt their potential. However, we must proceed with caution and wisdom. Here are some practical tips for those interested in this field:

1. **Stay informed:** The field is advancing at an incredible pace. Make it a habit to read the latest research papers and attend conferences. Networking with experts can open doors you never imagined.

2. **Learn the basics of neuroscience:** Understanding the brain is crucial. If possible, take some neurobiology courses. A solid foundation in neuroscience will deepen your appreciation of the complexities of brain function.

3. **Gain hands-on experience:** Many universities now host neuromorphic computing labs. Seek an internship or research position. The practical experience will be invaluable as you navigate this field.

4. **Consider ethics:** Always think about the ethical implications of your work. Ethics is not just about what we can do, but what we should do. Engage in discussions about ethics with your peers and mentors.

5. **Collaborate:** This field requires expertise from various disciplines. Build a diverse network of colleagues. Interdisciplinary collaboration often produces the best ideas.

As we continue to push the boundaries of what's possible, I can't help but feel a mix of excitement and trepidation. We're on the verge of fundamentally changing how we interact with technology and even how we understand ourselves. It's a responsibility we can't take lightly. Ultimately, the goal isn't just to create more intelligent machines and enhance human cognition. It's about making tools that help us think, learn, and grow. If we can strike that balance, the future looks bright indeed. But it's going to take a lot of hard work and careful thought to get there. Trust me, I've been in this game long enough to know it won't be easy. So, let's embrace this journey together. The path ahead may be fraught with challenges, but the discoveries waiting for us are bound to be nothing short of revolutionary. Each step we take brings us closer to understanding the technology and ourselves. It's a thrilling time to be involved in this field, and I hope you're as excited as I am about the possibilities that lie ahead.

# CHAPTER 15

## QUANTUM COMPUTING AND AI THE NEXT FRONTIER

*"Artificial intelligence is the science of making machines do things that would require intelligence if done by humans."* — **John McCarthy.**

As we stand on the brink of a technological revolution, few fields promise to profoundly reshape our understanding of computation and intelligence, such as **quantum computing** and **artificial intelligence (AI)**. This topic has been discussed for as long as I can remember. With over thirty years of experience in cybersecurity, I've witnessed many innovations, yet the fusion of these two domains feels like a leap into uncharted territory. It's a thrilling time to explore how quantum computing might revolutionize AI capabilities and applications.

### The Basics of Quantum Computing

To appreciate quantum computing's potential, we must first understand what it is. Unlike classical computers, which use bits as the smallest unit of data (0s and 1s), quantum computers utilize quantum bits, or **qubits**. Thanks to a phenomenon known as **superposition**, qubits can exist in multiple states at once. This allows quantum computers to process vast amounts of information simultaneously, making them exponentially more powerful than their classical counterparts for specific tasks.

I remember the first time I learned about the concept of superposition. During a conference, the speaker illustrated how a qubit could represent both 0 and 1 simultaneously. It felt like a light bulb went off in my head. The implications were staggering. If we could harness this power, we could solve problems currently intractable for classical computers.

Another fundamental principle of quantum computing is **entanglement**. When qubits become entangled, the state of one qubit is directly related to the state of another, no matter how far apart they are. This interconnectedness enables quantum computers to perform complex calculations that would take classical computers an impractical amount of time. The combination of superposition and entanglement gives quantum computers the potential to revolutionize fields ranging from cryptography to drug discovery.

## Quantum Computing Meets AI

Now, let's explore how quantum computing can enhance AI capabilities. One of the most promising applications is in **machine learning**. Traditional machine learning algorithms often struggle with large datasets, requiring significant computational resources and time. Quantum computing, with its ability to process multiple possibilities simultaneously, could significantly reduce the time needed to train AI models.

For instance, consider a scenario where an AI system recognizes patterns in vast datasets, such as images or speech. Classical algorithms might take hours or even days to analyze the data. In contrast, quantum algorithms could perform the same analysis in a fraction of the time. This capability could lead to breakthroughs like **image recognition**, **natural language processing**, and **predictive analytics**. I recall a project I worked on involving image recognition. We were using classical algorithms, and the processing time was excruciatingly slow. The idea of quantum computing speeding up that process was exciting. Imagine being able to analyze thousands of images in seconds rather than hours! It's a game-changer.

Additionally, quantum computing could enhance AI's capability to tackle **complex optimization problems**. Many real-world applications, such as logistics, finance, and drug discovery, require finding the best solution among numerous possibilities. Quantum algorithms, like the **Quantum Approximate Optimization Algorithm (QAOA)**, can explore these options more efficiently than classical algorithms. This could lead to more effective solutions in a shorter time, ultimately transforming industries.

## Revolutionizing Generative AI

Another exciting area where quantum computing could significantly impact is **generative AI**. Generative AI involves algorithms that create new content, such as images, music, or text, based on patterns learned from existing data. The computational power of quantum systems could enhance the capabilities of generative models, allowing them to produce more complex and realistic outputs.

For instance, envision a quantum-enhanced generative model that composes music resonating with human emotions. The potential applications are vast, ranging from entertainment to art and therapeutic uses. I often contemplate how this technology could transform the creative landscape. As someone who appreciates the arts, I find collaborating with AI to create something beautiful exceptionally appealing.

## Real-Time Applications and Emotion Detection

Quantum computing also holds promise for real-time applications, particularly in areas like **emotion detection**. AI systems capable of accurately interpreting human emotions have the potential to revolutionize customer service, mental health support, and even personal relationships. Quantum computing could enhance these systems' capabilities, enabling them to process emotional data more effectively.

For instance, consider a customer service AI capable of detecting customer frustration in their voice during a call. With quantum computing, this AI could analyze emotional nuances in real-time, adapting its responses to better meet the customer's needs. This level of responsiveness could enhance customer satisfaction and loyalty.

I recall a time when I felt frustrated with a customer service representative. If the AI had been able to sense my emotions and adjust its approach, it might have altered the interaction. The potential for quantum-enhanced emotion detection is not merely theoretical; it could have real-world implications for enhancing human interactions with technology.

## Challenges and Ethical Considerations

Despite the immense potential of quantum computing and AI, we must also acknowledge the challenges ahead. The technology is still in its infancy, and practical applications remain limited. Building stable quantum computers that operate reliably is a significant hurdle. Quantum systems are sensitive to their environment, and maintaining coherence among qubits is complex.

Furthermore, as we explore the intersection of quantum computing and AI, ethical considerations must be at the forefront of our discussions. The power of these technologies raises questions about privacy, security, and the potential for misuse. For instance, if quantum computing enables AI systems to process personal data more efficiently, how can we protect this data? The implications for surveillance and data privacy are profound.

I often reflect on our ethical dilemmas as we advance in this field. The responsibility that comes with developing powerful technologies cannot be overstated. We must engage in thoughtful discussions about the implications of our work and strive to create frameworks that prioritize ethical considerations.

## The Road Ahead

Despite the challenges, I remain optimistic about the future of quantum computing and AI. These technologies have tremendous potential to revolutionize our world. As we continue to push the boundaries of what is possible, I encourage those interested in this field to stay informed and engaged.

Here are some practical tips for navigating this exciting frontier:

1. **Stay curious:** The field of quantum computing is evolving rapidly. Make it a habit to read the latest research papers and attend conferences to remain updated on advancements.

2. **Learn the fundamentals:** It is essential to grasp the principles of quantum mechanics. To establish a strong foundation, consider enrolling in courses in quantum physics or quantum computing.

3. **Gain hands-on experience:** Many universities and research institutions are exploring quantum computing. To obtain practical experience, pursue internships or research opportunities.

4. **Engage in interdisciplinary collaboration:** Quantum computing and AI intersect with various fields, including physics, computer science, and ethics. Developing a diverse network of colleagues can lead to innovative ideas and solutions.

5. **Consider the ethical implications:** As you explore this field, always take into account the ethical considerations of your work. Discuss the societal impact of quantum computing and AI.

As we embark on this journey into the next frontier of technology, I can't help but feel a mix of excitement and responsibility. We are on the verge of fundamentally changing how we understand computation and intelligence. The discoveries awaiting us are sure to be nothing short of revolutionary.

Ultimately, the goal is to create more intelligent machines and enhance human cognition. If we can strike that balance, the future looks bright indeed. However, getting there will require hard work and careful thought. The potential rewards are worth every effort. Let's embrace this journey together and explore the incredible possibilities.

Here are some valuable references and resources related to quantum computing that can enhance your understanding of the topic:

1. **Books on Quantum Information**: A foundational text is *"The Physics of Quantum Information,"* edited by Bouwmeester, Ekert, and Zeilinger. This book offers a comprehensive overview of the principles underlying quantum information theory and its applications.

2. **Wikipedia Overview**: The Wikipedia page on quantum computing offers a comprehensive overview of the field, detailing the fundamental principles, the distinctions between classical and quantum computers, and the latest technological advancements.

3. **Historical Context**: From a historical perspective, *Carlo Rovelli's Helgoland* discusses the development of quantum theory and its implications for our understanding of reality, providing context for the evolution of quantum computing.

4. **Quantum Programming**: Resources such as the Qiskit documentation provide programming references and tutorials for individuals interested in developing quantum algorithms. Qiskit is an open-source quantum computing framework that enables users to create and execute quantum programs.

5. **Research Articles**: Various research articles examine specific aspects of quantum computing, including error mitigation strategies and the necessity of entanglement for quantum speedup. These articles explore the technical challenges and advancements in the field.

These are some reference materials I used while writing this book. They offer a mix of theoretical foundations, practical applications, and current research trends in quantum computing, making them valuable for anyone wanting to explore this exciting frontier.

# CHAPTER 16

## AI in Smart Cities: Urban Planning and Management

*"AI will not replace jobs, but it will change the nature of work." – **Kai-Fu Lee***

As urban populations continue to grow, the need for innovative solutions to manage city life has never been more urgent. **Artificial Intelligence (AI)** is emerging as a transformative force in shaping future cities, influencing everything from traffic management to energy distribution. Integrating AI into urban planning and management is not just a trend; it signifies a fundamental shift in how we conceive and operate our urban environments.

## The Role of AI in Urban Planning

AI is revolutionizing urban planning by providing valuable insights derived from data analysis. Traditional urban planning often relied on static models and historical data, which could lead to inefficiencies and outdated strategies. In contrast, AI enables planners to analyze vast amounts of real-time data, allowing for more dynamic and responsive decision-making. For instance, AI algorithms can process data from various sources, including traffic sensors, social media, and environmental monitoring systems, to identify patterns and predict future urban challenges. One of the most exciting applications of AI in urban planning is the development of **urban digital twins**. These virtual replicas of physical cities integrate real-time data to simulate and analyze urban dynamics. By using AI to create and maintain these digital twins, city planners can visualize the impact of potential changes before implementing them. This capability allows for more informed decisions regarding infrastructure development, zoning regulations, and resource allocation.

## Traffic Management and Mobility Solutions

Traffic congestion is a significant challenge in urban areas, leading to wasted time, increased pollution, and decreased quality of life. AI is crucial in addressing these issues through advanced traffic management systems. AI can optimize real-time traffic flow by analyzing traffic cameras, GPS devices, and social media data. For example, AI algorithms can adjust traffic signal timings based on current conditions, reducing wait times and improving overall traffic efficiency. Moreover, AI enhances mobility solutions by developing smart transportation systems. Ride-sharing platforms, autonomous vehicles, and public transit systems increasingly leverage AI to improve service delivery. AI can analyze user demand patterns, optimize routes, and even predict peak travel times, ensuring that transportation resources are allocated efficiently. This not only enhances the user experience but also contributes to reducing the carbon footprint of urban transportation.

## Energy Distribution and Sustainability

Energy management is another critical area where AI is making a significant impact. As cities strive for sustainability, AI technologies are being employed to optimize energy distribution and consumption. Smart grids powered by AI can analyze energy usage patterns and adjust supply accordingly. This capability allows for better integration of renewable energy sources, such as solar and wind, into the urban energy mix. AI can also facilitate energy efficiency in buildings. By analyzing data from sensors embedded in smart buildings, AI systems can optimize heating, cooling, and lighting based on occupancy and environmental conditions. This reduces energy consumption and lowers operational costs for building owners. For instance, AI-driven systems can automatically adjust heating and cooling settings in response to real-time occupancy data, ensuring that energy is used only when needed.

## Enhancing Public Safety and Emergency Response

Public safety is a paramount concern for urban planners, and AI is proving to be a valuable ally in this area. AI-powered surveillance systems can analyze video feeds in real time to detect unusual behavior or potential threats. This capability allows law enforcement agencies to respond more quickly to incidents, enhancing overall public safety. In addition to surveillance, AI can improve emergency response systems. By analyzing data from various sources, including social media and emergency calls, AI can help dispatchers prioritize responses and allocate resources more effectively. For example, AI can analyze real-time data during a natural disaster to identify the most affected areas and direct emergency services accordingly. This proactive approach can save lives and minimize damage during critical situations.

## Urban Resilience and Climate Adaptation

As cities face the growing threat of climate change, AI is crucial for enhancing urban resilience. AI systems can analyze environmental data to predict climate-related risks like flooding or heat waves. This information is invaluable for urban planners as they develop strategies to mitigate these risks and adapt to changing conditions. For instance, AI can help identify areas that are particularly vulnerable to flooding and inform decisions regarding infrastructure improvements, such as the construction of levees or the redesign of drainage systems. By leveraging AI to model potential climate scenarios, cities can proactively implement measures to protect their residents and infrastructure.

## Challenges and Ethical Considerations

While the potential of AI in smart cities is immense, it is essential to acknowledge the challenges and ethical considerations that accompany its implementation. Data privacy is a significant concern, as the collection and analysis of personal data can lead to potential misuse. Urban planners must ensure that data is collected and used responsibly, with appropriate safeguards in place to protect citizens' privacy. Moreover, the reliance on AI systems raises questions about accountability and transparency. As AI algorithms make decisions impacting urban life, it is crucial to ensure that these systems are fair and unbiased. Engaging with communities and stakeholders in the development of AI solutions can help address these concerns and foster trust in the technology.

## The Future of AI in Smart Cities

Looking ahead, the integration of AI into urban planning and management is set to reshape future cities. As technology continues to advance, we can anticipate even more innovative applications of AI that enhance urban living. From optimizing resource allocation to improving public services, AI holds the promise of creating more sustainable, efficient, and livable cities. To fully realize this potential, collaboration among various stakeholders is crucial. City governments, technology companies, and community organizations must unite to develop AI solutions that address the unique challenges of urban areas. By fostering a collaborative approach, we can ensure that AI serves as a tool for positive change in our cities.

In conclusion, AI represents a technological advancement and acts as a catalyst for transforming urban planning and management. As we embrace AI's possibilities in smart cities, we must remain vigilant in addressing the ethical considerations and the challenges that arise. By doing so, we can create urban environments that are not only smarter but also more inclusive and resilient for future generations. The journey toward smarter cities is just beginning, and the potential for innovation is limitless.

# CHAPTER 17:

## The Accelerating Pace of Technology and the Future of AI

*The ever-accelerating progress of technology and changes in the mode of human life give the appearance of approaching some essential singularity in the history of the race beyond which human affairs, as we know them, could not continue," -* **Ray Kurzweil**

The pace at which technology advances is nothing short of extraordinary. Innovation has consistently reshaped the world from the Industrial Revolution to the digital age. However, technological progress has become exponential in recent decades. This exponential growth is particularly evident in artificial intelligence (AI), which is evolving at an unprecedented rate and transforming industries, economies, and societies. In this chapter, we examine the rapid acceleration of technology, the timeline for AI's autonomy, and key predictions about how AI will shape the future.

## The Speed of Technological Progress

The concept of exponential growth in technology, epitomized by **Moore's Law**, has been a driving force behind the rapid increase in computing power. This law, which predicted that the number of transistors on a microchip would double approximately every two years, has historically fueled innovations across virtually every field. While Moore's Law has slowed in recent years due to physical limitations, advancements in other areas, particularly AI, continue accelerating.

## Key Drivers of AI Advancement

AI's rapid progress can be attributed to three primary factors:

1.  **Massive Data Availability**: The surge of digital devices, online activities, and connected sensors has generated vast datasets that power machine learning models.

2.  **Computational Power**: Enhancements in hardware, including GPUs (Graphics Processing Units) and TPUs (Tensor Processing Units), have allowed AI to process complex datasets at unprecedented speeds.

3.  **Algorithmic Breakthroughs**: Advances in machine learning, especially deep learning, have enabled AI systems to perform more sophisticated tasks, ranging from natural language understanding to image recognition.

As a result, AI has emerged as one of the most transformative technologies of our time. Its impact is expected to be staggering, with AI projected to contribute a monumental $15.7 trillion to the global economy by 2030. This revolution will not only reshape industries but also significantly change the global workforce.

## When Will AI Become Autonomous?

The timeline for AI to achieve full autonomy is a subject of significant debate among researchers and technologists. The answer depends on the definition of "autonomy," as AI is already autonomous in specific domains but is still far from achieving general autonomy across all areas of human activity.

## Domain-Specific Autonomy

AI systems can already operate autonomously in well-defined and controlled environments. For example:

- **Industrial manufacturing and logistics**: Robots and AI systems automate tasks such as assembly, quality control, and inventory management without human intervention.

- **Autonomous Vehicles and Drones**: Self-driving cars and drones are advancing rapidly; however, they still require human oversight in unpredictable or complex scenarios.

These domain-specific applications illustrate that AI is making significant progress toward achieving autonomy, yet its capabilities are still confined to narrow, specialized tasks.

## General Autonomy

Achieving **general AI autonomy**, where AI can perform any intellectual task a human can without human intervention, remains a distant goal. Experts disagree on when—or even if—this level of AI will be achieved. Predictions range from the 2040s to the end of the century, depending on the technical and ethical challenges that must be addressed.

## Challenges to Autonomy

Several obstacles must be overcome before AI can achieve widespread autonomy:

1. **Trust and reliability**: AI systems must consistently demonstrate performance and reliability across diverse and unpredictable scenarios.

2. **Ethical Considerations**: Addressing bias, ensuring transparency, and establishing accountability in AI decision-making is paramount. This is crucial to guarantee that AI systems are designed and used in ways that align with human values and do not perpetuate or exacerbate existing biases.

3. **Regulatory Frameworks**: Governments and organizations must establish clear guidelines for the use of autonomous AI, especially in sensitive areas such as healthcare, law enforcement, and transportation.

## Predictions for the Future of AI

The future of AI is filled with possibilities. Based on current trends, here are key predictions about how AI will shape businesses, societies, and industries:

### AI's Role in Business and Industry

- **Automation and Efficiency**: AI will continue to automate repetitive and labor-intensive tasks, enhancing efficiency and lowering costs across industries such as manufacturing, customer service, and logistics.

- **Personalized Experiences**: Businesses will leverage AI to provide hyper-personalized products and services, customizing offerings to suit individual preferences and behaviors.

- **Generative AI Expansion**: Generative AI technologies, such as those used to create text, images, and videos, will grow more sophisticated and transformative, revolutionizing creative industries.

## Societal and Ethical Impacts

- **Human-Centered AI**: A shift toward ethical, human-centered AI development will ensure that systems are designed to align with societal values and address biases. This approach will make the audience feel valued and integral to AI development.

- **Job Displacement and Creation**: While AI will automate many tasks, it will also create new roles in AI development, maintenance, and oversight, providing reassurance about the future of work. Workforce training and education will be vital for navigating this transition.

- **Regulation and Governance**: Governments will increasingly implement regulations to ensure responsible AI usage and address concerns regarding privacy, security, and misuse.

## Autonomous AI Systems

- **Autonomous Machines**: Self-driving vehicles, drones, and other autonomous systems will become increasingly reliable and more widely adopted. However, achieving full autonomy in complex environments will require overcoming significant challenges.

- **Transformative AI**: By the 2030s or 2040s, some experts predict the emergence of transformative AI capable of performing tasks across various domains with minimal human intervention. However, this remains speculative.

## AI in Healthcare and Science

- **Revolutionizing Healthcare**: AI will play a crucial role in diagnosing diseases, developing personalized treatments, and accelerating drug discovery. These advancements could greatly enhance global health outcomes.

- **Scientific Discovery**: AI's capacity to analyze extensive datasets will propel advancements in areas such as climate modeling, neuroscience, and materials science.

## Long-Term Predictions

- **AI as a Collaborative Partner**: By 2035, AI is anticipated to serve as a collaborative partner for humans, enhancing creativity, decision-making, and problem-solving rather than completely replacing human roles.

- **Potential Risks**: Experts caution about potential dangers, including malicious actors misusing AI, privacy loss, and the likelihood of AI worsening social inequalities if not managed carefully.

# Quantum Computing and the Future of Cybersecurity

Another area we already discussed is related to the future of AI: quantum computing, which has the potential to revolutionize cybersecurity, both as a threat and a safeguard.

## Threats to Cybersecurity

- **Breaking Encryption**: Quantum computers may make current encryption methods obsolete by solving complex mathematical problems at an exponential speed compared to classical computers.

- **AI-Driven Cyberattacks**: AI could be weaponized to automate and enhance cyberattacks, creating more sophisticated phishing attempts, malware, and system infiltrations.

## Opportunities for Enhanced Cybersecurity

- **Quantum-Resistant Cryptography**: Researchers are creating new encryption algorithms designed to withstand quantum computing attacks, thereby ensuring the security of sensitive data.

- **AI-Augmented Defenses**: AI analyzes real-time data to detect and proactively respond to cyber threats, enhancing overall security measures.

- **Quantum Cryptography**: Quantum key distribution (QKD) provides theoretically unbreakable encryption, paving the way for more secure communication systems.

## Preparing for the Future

The rapid pace of technological advancement demands proactive preparation. To successfully navigate the challenges and opportunities presented by AI and quantum computing, organizations and governments must:

1. **Invest in Workforce Training**: Equip individuals with the skills necessary to thrive in an AI-driven economy.

2. **Adopt post-quantum security measures**: Transition to quantum-resistant encryption methods to protect sensitive information.

3. **Establish Ethical Guidelines**: Set standards for the responsible use of AI and quantum technologies.

4. **Foster Global Collaboration**: Collaborate to create governance frameworks that ensure technology serves humanity.

The exponential pace of technological progress, particularly in AI, is reshaping the world at an unprecedented rate. From domain-specific autonomy to transformative AI, the future holds immense potential, yet it also faces significant challenges. By fostering collaboration, prioritizing ethical development, and preparing for change, we can harness technology's transformative power while mitigating its risks. The future is not just about advancing technology—it's about ensuring that advancements serve humanity's best interests.

# CONCLUSION

## THE ROAD AHEAD

*"AI will change the nature of creativity, so we must develop new ways to interact with these machines." –* **Yves Behar**

We've explored how artificial intelligence (AI) is reshaping industries, revolutionizing business, and opening up new frontiers in science and technology. But where does that leave us? The road ahead for AI is filled with **promise and uncertainty**, and our choices today will shape its impact on society for decades.

As AI advances, we need to ask ourselves a few key questions: How do we ensure that AI serves humanity rather than dominates it? How can we create a world where humans and machines work harmoniously? And most importantly, how do we build an AI-driven future that is ethical, inclusive, and sustainable?

Let's take a step back and examine some of the major insights we gained from our journey through the world of AI.

### AI's Transformative Potential

At its core, AI is a powerful tool capable of addressing some of the world's most pressing challenges. Whether it's improving healthcare, fighting climate change, or boosting economic productivity, AI has the potential to create a real difference in people's lives. However, it's important to remember that AI is not a solution in and of itself; it's a means to an end. The way we use AI will determine its true value.

Take healthcare, for example. AI has the potential to revolutionize diagnostics, streamline treatment plans, and bring healthcare to underserved communities. However, to unlock this potential, we must ensure that the systems we build are accurate, fair, and accessible to everyone. Without careful planning and oversight, AI could exacerbate inequalities instead of reducing them.

The same applies to fields such as education, business, and environmental sustainability. AI presents remarkable opportunities, but it also entails risks. To fully harness AI's transformative potential, we must engage with it responsibly and thoughtfully.

## The Importance of Ethics and Transparency

One of the most essential lessons from our exploration of AI is the need for ethical guidelines and transparency. As AI becomes more integrated into our daily lives, the decisions made by these systems directly impact individuals, communities, and entire societies. AI systems must be designed to be **fair, transparent, and accountable**.

Consider **bias** in AI systems. If left unchecked, bias in data and algorithms can result in discriminatory outcomes in fields like hiring, lending, or law enforcement. However, we can mitigate these risks by identifying the potential for bias early and implementing fairness checks throughout the AI development process.

Transparency is equally important. People need to understand how AI systems work, how decisions are made, and what data is being used. This is especially crucial in high-stakes environments like healthcare or criminal justice, where lives and livelihoods are at stake. Building trust in AI involves ensuring that these systems are **explainable** and that their decision-making processes are visible to those affected.

## Human-Centered AI: The Path Forward

One of the central themes in our discussion has been **human-centered AI**—an approach that prioritizes collaboration between humans and machines. Instead of viewing AI as a replacement for human workers, we should see it as a partner that enhances our capabilities.

This involves designing AI systems that enhance human strengths while allowing space for human judgment, creativity, and emotional intelligence. AI can manage repetitive tasks and analyze large datasets, but it lacks the empathy, intuition, and nuance that humans possess. **Human-AI collaboration** is crucial to ensuring that AI enhances, rather than diminishes, the human experience.

This involves investing in **education and training** programs that prepare workers for an AI-driven future. Reskilling and upskilling initiatives will assist people in transitioning to new roles that leverage both human and AI strengths. The future of work is not about choosing between humans and machines—it's about discovering ways for the two to collaborate in synergy.

## Global Cooperation and Governance

AI's influence extends far beyond individual countries or industries. It's a global phenomenon that demands **international cooperation**. As nations compete to develop AI technologies, there's a significant risk of creating a fragmented world where AI regulations, standards, and ethical norms differ greatly.

That's why countries must collaborate to establish **global AI governance frameworks**. These frameworks should tackle issues such as data privacy, security, ethical AI use, and the potential for AI to be weaponized. International bodies like the United Nations, the OECD, and other organizations have already initiated these discussions, but there's still a long road ahead.

The future of AI will be shaped not only by technological advancements but also by the policies, regulations, and ethical standards we implement. This necessitates a commitment to **collaboration** at the global level—between governments, businesses, and civil society.

## Embracing AI with a Sense of Purpose

As we look to the future, it's important to remember that AI ultimately reflects the people who build and use it. If we design AI systems to improve lives, address societal challenges, and create a more equitable world, that's the future we'll make. However, if we ignore the ethical implications and allow AI to be driven solely by profit or power, we risk a future where technology harms more than it helps.

The road ahead for AI is full of promise, but it is also filled with uncertainty. It is up to us—researchers, policymakers, business leaders, and everyday citizens—to **shape AI's future** in a manner that aligns with our values. Doing so can ensure that AI becomes a force for good in the world.

## Final Thoughts

Artificial intelligence is no longer merely a futuristic concept—it's here and already transforming how we live and work. However, with that power comes responsibility. As we advance into this AI-driven future, we must approach it with **purpose, caution, and optimism.**

Our choices today will determine whether AI becomes a tool that uplifts humanity or divides us. By prioritizing ethics, transparency, collaboration, and global cooperation, we can ensure that AI serves the greater good and helps build a future that benefits everyone.

The road ahead is long, but it is also filled with opportunity. Let us embrace AI with open eyes and hearts, and together, let us build a future where humans and machines work together to create a better world for all.

# GLOSSARY OF TERMS

1. **AI (Artificial Intelligence):** The simulation of human intelligence processes by machines, particularly computer systems. This includes learning, reasoning, and self-correction capabilities.
2. **Algorithm:** A computer follows a process or set of rules in calculations or problem-solving operations, particularly in AI, to process data and make decisions.
3. **Automata:** Mechanical devices capable of automatically performing a series of actions are often considered early forms of robots or AI due to their ability to mimic human or animal actions.
4. **Bias in AI:** Systematic and unfair discrimination in AI algorithms often results from biased training data or flawed assumptions in model design.
5. **Cybersecurity:** The practice of protecting systems, networks, and programs from digital attacks, unauthorized access, damage, or disruption.
6. **Deep Learning:** A subset of machine learning involving neural networks with many layers, which allows computers to learn from vast amounts of data, is often used in creating deepfakes and other advanced AI applications.
7. **Deepfakes:** AI-generated media in which a person in an existing image or video is replaced with someone else's likeness is often used maliciously to mislead or deceive.
8. **Entanglement**: A quantum mechanical phenomenon in which two or more quantum particles become interlinked, such that the state of one particle cannot be described independently of the others, even if a considerable distance separates them.
9. **Explainable AI (XAI)**: The field of AI focuses on making the decision-making processes of AI systems more interpretable and understandable to human users.
10. **Generative AI:** A subset of artificial intelligence that focuses on creating new content, including images, text, or audio, by learning patterns from existing data.
11. **Generative Adversarial Networks (GANs):** A class of machine learning frameworks where two neural networks, a generator, and a discriminator, compete against each other to

produce increasingly realistic data, often used in creating deepfakes.

12. **Human-Centered AI:** An approach to AI development that prioritizes human needs and values, ensuring AI technologies complement rather than replace human capabilities.

13. **LIME (Local Interpretable Model-agnostic Explanations):** This technique explains the predictions of any machine learning classifier by approximating it locally with an interpretable model.

14. **Machine Learning:** A type of AI that allows software applications to become more accurate at predicting outcomes without being explicitly programmed to do so, relying on patterns and inference instead.

15. **Neural Networks:** Deep learning uses computational models inspired by the human brain, which consists of interconnected nodes that process information in layers.

16. **Privacy Law:** Legal frameworks designed to protect personal information and data privacy often intersect with AI due to its reliance on data collection and processing.

17. **Quantum Computing:** A type of computing that utilizes the principles of quantum mechanics, such as superposition and entanglement, to perform computations fundamentally different from classical computers.

18. **Quantum Bits (Qubits):** A quantum computer's basic unit of information can exist in multiple states simultaneously, unlike the binary bits (0 and 1) used in classical computers.

19. **SHAP (SHapley Additive exPlanations):** A method for explaining any machine learning model's output by computing each feature's contribution to a particular prediction.

20. **Superintelligence:** A hypothetical form of AI that surpasses human intelligence in all fields, including creativity, general wisdom, and social skills, posing potential ethical and existential risks.

21. **Superposition:** A fundamental principle in quantum mechanics is that a quantum system can exist in multiple states simultaneously rather than being limited to a single state.

22. **Turing Test:** A test proposed by Alan Turing to determine a machine's ability to exhibit intelligent behavior equivalent to, or indistinguishable from, that of a human.

23. **Transparency:** The practice of making AI systems understandable and their decisions explainable to users is crucial for building trust and accountability in AI applications.

24. **Upskilling:** The process of teaching current employees new skills to help them work with AI technologies effectively and ensure they can adapt to changing job requirements.

25. **Variational Autoencoders (VAEs):** A type of generative model that learns to encode data into a latent space and then decode it back to the original data, enabling the generation of new data points.

26. **Watermarking Technologies:** Techniques used to embed information into digital media to verify authenticity and trace the origin are often employed to combat the misuse of deepfakes.

# INDEX

# REFERENCES & RESOURCES

*AI And The Future Of Work: Will Robots Replace Human Workers? | Blue Headline. (2023, March 17). Blue Headline.* https://blueheadline.com/need-to-know/ai-and-the-future-of-work-will-robots-replace-human-workers/

*Bennett. (2024, May 5). Secure Your Future with AI Data Privacy Assurance. Press Report.* https://press-report.net/ai-news/ai-in-business/ai-data-privacy-assurance/

*Bharat. (2023, September 20). Exploring the 7 Types of AI in 2023: Navigating the Artificial Intelligence Landscape. OpenCV.* https://opencv.org/blog/exploring-the-7-types-of-ai/

*Bokhovkin, A., & Burnaev, E. (2019). Boundary Loss for Remote Sensing Imagery Semantic Segmentation. ArXiv.org.* https://arxiv.org/abs/1905.07852. *A unified approach to interpreting model predictions. Proceedings of the 36th International Conference on Machine Learning (ICML), 97, 13071-13080.*

*Bostrom, N. (2014). Superintelligence: Paths, Dangers, Strategies. Oxford University Press.*

*Bouwmeester, D., Ekert, A. K, & Zeilinger, A. (2011). The physics of quantum information : quantum cryptography, quantum teleportation, quantum computation. Springer.*

*Campbell, A. (2023, December 5). Shanghai's Push for AI: Microsoft's Role in Boosting Businesses. Baseline.* https://www.baselinemag.com/news/shanghais-push-for-ai-microsofts-role-in-boosting-businesses/

*Chalmers, D. (2010). The singularity: A philosophical analysis.* https://consc.net/papers/singularity.pdf

*Chalmers, D. J. (n.d.). Facing Up to the Problem of Consciousness. Consc.net. Retrieved October 2, 2022, from* https://consc.net/papers/facing.html. *Journal of Consciousness Studies 2(3):200-19, 1995.*

*Chalmers, D. J. (1996). The Conscious Mind: In Search of a Fundamental Theory. Oxford University Press.*

Chalmers, D. J. (1999). The Hard Problem of Consciousness." *Journal of Consciousness Studies, vol. 2, no. 3, pp. 200–219. Consc.* https://consc.net/papers/facing.pdf

Chesterman, S. (2020). *ARTIFICIAL INTELLIGENCE AND THE LIMITS OF LEGAL PERSONALITY. International and Comparative Law Quarterly, 69(4), 819–844.* https://doi.org/10.1017/s0020589320000366

Christensen, J. (2023, August 1). *AI-supported mammogram screening increases breast cancer detection by 20%, study finds. CNN.* https://www.cnn.com/2023/08/01/health/ai-breast-cancer-detection/index.html

Çıtak, E. (2023, June 15). *How artificial intelligence went from fiction to science? Dataconomy.* https://dataconomy.com/2023/06/15/timeline-of-artificial-intelligence/

Collymore, L. (2023, July 9). *The Dark Side of Machine Learning: The Risks and Ethical Concerns. Blogspot.com; Blogger.* https://aibeekpassion.blogspot.com/2023/07/the-dark-side-of-machine-learning-risks.html

Company, R. (2024, January 25). *Exploring American Perceptions: Will AI Revolutionize the Workforce? Reekolect™.* https://www.reekolectcorp.com/post/exploring-american-perceptions-will-ai-revolutionize-the-workforce

COMPAS (software). (2020, July 11). *Wikipedia.* https://en.wikipedia.org/wiki/COMPAS_(software)

Daniel Clement Dennett. (1991). *Consciousness explained. Little, Brown and Company.*

Desurvire, E. (2009). *Classical and Quantum Information Theory. Cambridge University Press.*

EU AI Act: first regulation on artificial intelligence. (2023, June 8). *European Parliament.* https://www.europarl.europa.eu/topics/en/article/20230601STO93804/eu-ai-act-first-regulation-on-artificial-intelligence

European Union. (2021, September 7). *The EU Artificial Intelligence Act. The Artificial Intelligence Act.* https://artificialintelligenceact.eu/

Farhi, E., Goldstone, J., Gutmann, S., & Zhou, L. (2022). *The Quantum Approximate Optimization Algorithm and the Sherrington-Kirkpatrick Model at Infinite Size. Quantum, 6, 759.* https://doi.org/10.22331/q-2022-07-07-759

Farrell, R. (2022). *Innopharma Education Blog. Default.* https://www.innopharmaeducation.com/our-blog/the-impact-of-ai-on-job-roles-workforce-and-employment-what-you-need-to-know

*Gen AI Integration in Businesses: Exploring the Potential and Possibilities.* (2023, September 25). Fractal. https://fractal.ai/genai/business-possibilities-with-generative-ai/

Gross, P. (2024, July 18). *States strike out on their own on AI, privacy regulation • Washington State Standard. Washington State Standard.* https://washingtonstatestandard.com/2024/07/18/states-strike-out-on-their-own-on-ai-privacy-regulation/

Hanna, S., Pither, J., & Vis-Dunbar, M. (2021). *Implementation of an Open Science Instruction Program for Undergraduates. Data Intelligence, 3(1), 150–161.* https://doi.org/10.1162/dint_a_00086

Hillary, & Scott-Briggs, A. (2023, October 28). *A Historical Dive into the Birth of Artificial Intelligence. TechBullion.* https://techbullion.com/a-historical-dive-into-the-birth-of-artificial-intelligence/

*I Object! How AI Could Challenge Legal Precedent.* (2015). Legalpdf.io. https://legalpdf.io/blog/i_object_how_ai_could_challenge_legal_precedent.php

*IEEE Ethics In Action in Autonomous and Intelligent Systems | IEEE SA.* (n.d.). *Ethics in Action | Ethically Aligned Design.* https://ethicsinaction.ieee.org/

innovationthings. (2023, July 29). *Brain–Computer Interfaces (BCIs) - INNOVATIONTHINGS. INNOVATIONTHINGS.* http://innovationthings.com/brain-computer-interfaces-bcis/

Ioannou, L. M. (2007). *Computational complexity of the quantum separability problem. Quantum Information and Computation, 7(4), 336–370.* https://doi.org/10.26421/qic7.4-5

ISHANN BHARDWAJ. (2023). *Artificial Intelligence and its Patentability: A*

*Comparative Study Between India,UK, and USA. International Journal for Multidisciplinary Research, 5(3).* https://doi.org/10.36948/ijfmr.2023.v05i03.3666

John Gribbin. (2014). *Computing with quantum cats : from Colossus to Qubits.* Prometheus Books.

Kang, T. (2022). *Faculty of Engineering WEED RECOGNITION IN AGRICULTURE USING MASK R- CNN. In Core.* https://core.ac.uk/download/542313585.pdf

Kurbalija, J. (2023, August 1). *What can Socrates teach us about AI and prompting? - Humainism. Humainism.ai.* https://humainism.ai/blogs/what-can-socrates-teach-us-about-ai-and-prompting/

Kuźnar, M., & Lorenc, A. (2023). *A Hybrid Method for Technical Condition Prediction Based on AI as an Element for Reducing Supply Chain Disruptions. Applied Science, 13(22), 12439.* https://doi.org/10.3390/app132212439

Larson, J., Mattu, S., Kirchner, L., & Angwin, J. (2016, May 23). *How We Analyzed the COMPAS Recidivism Algorithm. ProPublica.* https://www.propublica.org/article/how-we-analyzed-the-compas-recidivism-algorithm

Lauren, L. (2024, April 25). *What Do Philosophers Say About Ultimate Reality? AfterQuotes.* https://afterquotes.com/what-do-philosophers-say-about-ultimate-reality/

Lipton, Z. C. (2017). *The Mythos of Model Interpretability.* https://arxiv.org/abs/1606.03490. *Proceedings of the 2016 ICML Workshop on Human Interpretability in Machine Learning.*

Liz Mineo. (2024, January 12). *"Killer robots" are coming, and U.N. is worried. Harvard Gazette.* https://news.harvard.edu/gazette/story/2024/01/killer-robots-are-coming-and-u-n-is-worried/

Market, L. (2024). *Emerging Technologies Leading Market Disruption - FasterCapital. FasterCapital.* https://fastercapital.com/content/Emerging-Technologies-Leading-Market-Disruption.html

Miller, T. (2019). *Explanation in artificial intelligence: Insights from the social sciences. Artificial Intelligence, 267, 1–38.* https://doi.org/10.1016/j.artint.2018.07.007

Nielsen, M. A., & Chuang, I. L. (2010). *Quantum Computation and Quantum Information*. Cambridge University Press.

Ogar, P. (2023, May 18). *The Real Dangers of Deepfake: Could it Undermine Society?* Metaroids. https://metaroids.com/learn/the-real-dangers-of-deepfake-could-it-undermine-society/

Ostrovsky, M. (2021, November 9). *Managing Ethical Challenges in an AI Environment*. Repustate.com; Repustate. https://www.repustate.com/blog/managing-ethical-challenges-ai/

Park, A. (2020). *Google's AI Bested Doctors in Detecting Breast Cancer in Mammograms*. Time; Time. https://time.com/5754183/google-ai-mammograms-breast-cancer/

Park, A. L. (2019, February 19). *Injustice Ex Machina: Predictive Algorithms in Criminal Sentencing*. UCLA Law Review. https://www.uclalawreview.org/injustice-ex-machina-predictive-algorithms-in-criminal-sentencing/

PCFixer. (2024, July 11). *Exploring the Future of Quantum Computing | PC Fixer*. PC Fixer. https://pcfixercomputerrepairs.co.uk/exploring-the-future-of-quantum-computing/

Pittenger, A. O. (2012). *An Introduction to Quantum Computing Algorithms*. Springer Science & Business Media.

PurpleSec. (2024, August 13). *Purplesec*. PurpleSec. https://purplesec.us/resources/cybersecurity-statistics/

Putnam, H. (2011). *Representation and reality*. MIT Press.

*Quantum Networking and Security - Q-R*. (2023, November 25). Q-R. https://www.qui-recherche.info/quantum-networking-and-security.html

Quill, H. (2024, July 17). *The Future of Humanity: Technological Advances and Societal Shifts*. Trending.com. https://trending.com/articles/lifestyle/the-future-of-humanity-technological-advances-and-societal-shifts

Ribeiro, M. T., Singh, S., & Guestrin, C. (2016, February 16). *"Why Should I Trust*

*You?": Explaining the Predictions of Any Classifier. ArXiv.org.*
*https://arxiv.org/abs/1602.04938*

Rickett, A. (2023, November 22). *The OpenAI Saga Continues: Sam Altman Returns? AI Smart Marketing.* https://aismartmarketing.com/the-openai-saga-continues-sam-altman-returns/

Riley Tipton Perry. (2012). *Quantum Computing from the Ground Up. World Scientific Publishing Company.*

Roser, M. (2023, February 22). *Technology over the long run: zoom out to see how dramatically the world can change within a lifetime. Our World in Data.* https://ourworldindata.org/technology-long-run

Rovelli, C. (2021). *Helgoland. Penguin Books.*

Russel, S., & Norvig, P. (2021). *Artificial intelligence: A Modern approach (4th ed.). Prentice Hall.*

S, N. (2024, February 12). *5 Things Privacy Professionals Should Consider At The Intersection of AI And Data Privacy. Hawkdive.com; Hawkdive Media.* https://www.hawkdive.com/5-things-privacy-professionals-should-consider-at-the-intersection-of-ai-and-data-privacy/

Samuel, A. L. (1959). *Some Studies in Machine Learning Using the Game of Checkers. IBM Journal of Research and Development, 3(3), 210–229.* https://doi.org/10.1147/rd.33.0210

Santanu Pattanayak. (2021). *Quantum machine learning with Python : using cirq from Google research and IBM Qiskit. Apress.*

Schneppat, J. O. (2023, September 6). *Quantum Computer & AI: The Future of Technology - "The AI Chronicles" Podcast. Buzzsprout.* https://gpt-5.buzzsprout.com/2193055/episodes/13531959

Siddiqui, A. R. (2023, December 7). *Deepfakes are Lurking in 2024 — Here's How to Unmask Them. Entrepreneur.* https://www.entrepreneur.com/leadership/deepfakesare-lurking-in-2024-heres-how-to-unmask-them/465720

Singh, S. (2023, January 16). *AI In Agriculture: Using Computer Vision To Improve Crop Yields -*. Analytics Vidhya. https://www.analyticsvidhya.com/blog/2023/01/ai-in-agriculture-using-computer-vision-to-improve-crop-yields/

Strickland, J. (2008, October 15). *What's the technological singularity?* HowStuffWorks. https://electronics.howstuffworks.com/gadgets/high-tech-gadgets/technological-singularity.htm

Team AIWS. (2020). *Preparing Future Innovators: Cultivating Ethical AI Understanding in Students | AIWS*. AIWS. https://aiworldschool.com/preparing-future-innovators-cultivating-ethical-ai-understanding-in-students/

Tegmark, M. (2015). *Benefits & Risks of Artificial Intelligence*. Future of Life Institute. https://futureoflife.org/background/benefits-risks-of-artificial-intelligence/

*The Ethical Dilemmas of Data Science: Balancing Privacy and Innovation | Covelent Insights*. (n.d.). Www.covelent.com. https://www.covelent.com/articles/the-ethical-dilemmas-of-data-science-balancing-privacy-with-innovation

Thomas X. Hammes. (2023, November 2). *Autonomous weapons are the moral choice*. Atlantic Council. https://www.atlanticcouncil.org/blogs/new-atlanticist/autonomous-weapons-are-the-moral-choice/

Tolan, P. (2024, July 5). *The EU AI Act: Will UK Employers Be Affected? AI Industry News*. https://roboticulized.com/uncategorized/2024/07/05/151100/the-eu-ai-act-will-uk-employers-be-affected/

Turing, A. (1950). *Computing Machinery and Intelligence*. Mind, 59(236), 433–460. https://doi.org/10.1093/mind/lix.236.433

*Understanding the workings of artificial intelligence*. (2024, January 24). Mmcalumni.ca. https://mmcalumni.ca/blog/how-artificial-intelligence-works-in-the-modern-world

Varela, F. J., Rosch, E., & Thompson, E. (2016). *The Embodied Mind : Cognitive science and human experience*. The Mit Press.

Venkata Tadi. (2021). *Navigating Ethical Challenges and Biases in Generative AI: Ensuring Trust and Fairness in B2B Sales Interactions and Decision-Making*. Journal of Artificial Intelligence & Cloud Computing, 3(2), 1–10.

*https://www.onlinescientificresearch.com/articles/navigating-ethical-challenges-and-biases-in-generative-ai-ensuring-trust-and-fairness-in-b2b-sales-interactions-and-decisionmaking.html*

Wallach, W., & Allen, C. (2010). *Moral machines : Teaching robots right from wrong.* Oxford University Press.

Weizenbaum, J. (1991). *Computer power and human reason : from judgment to calculation.* S.H. Freeman.

Whittaker, M., Crawford, K., Dobbe, R., Fried, G., Kaziunas, E., Mathur, V., West, S. M., Richardson, R., Schultz, J., & Schwartz, O. (2018). *AI Now Report 2018.* *https://ainowinstitute.org/wp-content/uploads/2023/04/AI_Now_2018_Report.pdf*

William, W. (2024, January 8). *The Next Frontier: Emerging Technologies Shaping the Future - 1mut. 1mut.* *https://1mut.com/the-next-frontier-emerging-technologies-shaping-the-future/*

XiXiDu. (2011, December 19). *Q&A with Michael Littman on risks from AI.* *Lesswrong.com.* *https://www.lesswrong.com/posts/j5ComXKhingWjqSgA/q-and-a-with-michael-littman-on-risks-from-ai*

Yanofsky, N. S., & Mannucci, M. A. (2008). *Quantum Computing for Computer Scientists.* Cambridge University Press.

# ABOUT THE AUTHOR

**Chad M. Barr**

Chad Barr is a distinguished Cybersecurity Executive Leader and visionary strategist with over two decades of experience in information security, technology, and artificial intelligence. Chad shares his expertise in educating others about cybersecurity and the intersection of AI with security practices via his blog.

Throughout his career, Chad has held pivotal roles that have shaped his comprehensive understanding of cybersecurity challenges across various industries. His experience spans diverse sectors, including retail, banking, real estate, healthcare, manufacturing, and government. This broad exposure has enabled Chad to develop and implement sustainable and resilient security frameworks tailored to specific industry needs, often leveraging cutting-edge AI technologies.

Chad's approach integrates cybersecurity strategy with governance, risk management, and compliance while incorporating AI-driven solutions. He excels in aligning security initiatives with business objectives, ensuring that security and AI are fundamental drivers of organizational success. His expertise includes strategic cybersecurity governance, risk management and mitigation, regulatory compliance leadership, artificial intelligence in cybersecurity, machine learning for threat detection, and security architecture and engineering.

As a thought leader in the field, Chad has contributed significantly to cybersecurity education and awareness, particularly in the realm of AI-enhanced security practices. He frequently speaks on AI's potential to revolutionize cybersecurity and its unique challenges.

Chad's credentials are as impressive as his experience. His extensive certification portfolio includes C|CISO, CISSP, CCSP, CCSK, CISA, and CDPSE, underscoring his comprehensive understanding of cybersecurity challenges. Additionally, Chad has pursued specialized training in AI and machine learning applications in cybersecurity.

Through his work, Chad continues to drive innovation in cybersecurity. He helps organizations navigate the complex landscape of digital threats while fostering a culture of security resilience. His strategic leadership, deep technical knowledge, and expertise in AI make him a trusted advisor and influential voice in the cybersecurity community, particularly in guiding the responsible and effective integration of AI technologies in security operations.

Connect with Chad:

- LinkedIn: https://www.linkedin.com/in/chadbarr/

- Personal Blog: https://www.chadmbarr.com/

# ALSO BY CHAD BARR

**Fortifying The Digital Castle**
https://chadmbarr.com/fortifying-the-digital-castle/


Watch for more at Chad Barr's site.
https://www.chadmbarr.com/

https://linktr.ee/chadbarr

Thank You for Reading!

Dear Reader,

I want to take a moment to thank you personally for picking up my book and spending your valuable time reading my story. Your support means the world to me, and I hope you enjoyed the journey as much as I enjoyed creating it.

If you loved the book (or even just liked it!), I'd be incredibly grateful if you could take a few minutes to leave a review on Amazon or wherever you purchased it. Your review not only helps me as an author but also helps other readers discover this book.

Whether it's a few words or a detailed review, every bit of feedback makes a huge difference. Thank you for being a part of my story, and I can't wait to share more adventures with you in the future!

With gratitude,

Chad Barr